794.8 Vid
Video games /

34028066779878
NC $19.95   ocn173243749
02/29/08

3 4028 06677 98
HARRIS COUNTY PUBLIC LIB

D1204702

At Issue

Video Games

Withdrawn
Print

Other Books in the At Issue Series:

At Issue

Video Games

David M. Haugen, Book Editor

GREENHAVEN PRESS

An imprint of Thomson Gale, a part of The Thomson Corporation

Detroit • New York • San Francisco • New Haven, Conn. • Waterville, Maine • London

Christine Nasso, *Publisher*
Elizabeth Des Chenes, *Managing Editor*

© 2008 The Gale Group.

Star logo is a trademark and Gale and Greenhaven Press are registered trademarks used herein under license.

For more information, contact:
Greenhaven Press
27500 Drake Rd.
Farmington Hills, MI 48331-3535
Or you can visit our Internet site at http://www.gale.com

ALL RIGHTS RESERVED
No part of this work covered by the copyright hereon may be reproduced or used in any form or by any means—graphic, electronic, or mechanical, including photocopying, recording, taping, Web distribution, or information storage retrieval systems—without the written permission of the publisher.

Articles in Greenhaven Press anthologies are often edited for length to meet page requirements. In addition, original titles of these works are changed to clearly present the main thesis and to explicitly indicate the author's opinion. Every effort is made to ensure that Greenhaven Press accurately reflects the original intent of the authors. Every effort has been made to trace the owners of copyrighted material.

LIBRARY OF CONGRESS CATALOGING-IN-PUBLICATION DATA

Video games / David M. Haugen, book editor.
   p. cm. -- (At issue)
Includes bibliographical references and index.
ISBN-13: 978-0-7377-3697-7 (hardcover)
ISBN-13: 978-0-7377-3698-4 (pbk.)
   1. Video games--Social aspects. I. Haugen, David M., 1969-
GV1469.34.S52V54 2008
794.8--dc22

2007037479

ISBN-10: 0-7377-3697-6 (hardcover)
ISBN-10: 0-7377-3698-4 (pbk.)

Printed in the United States of America
10 9 8 7 6 5 4 3 2 1

Contents

Introduction

Between their most recent peaks in 1993 and 2007, youth violence statistics in the United States steadily declined by more than 70 percent. This downtrend was seen as part of a continuing decline in youth violence rates since the 1970s. Over the same period, the video game industry charted an upward growth rate from a handful of enthusiasts creating simplistic two-dimensional, table tennis games such as Pong to numerous multi-billion-dollar software companies churning out three-dimensional games that have realistic, interactive environments and entail a good deal of role-playing. The inverse relationship between the evolution of video game sophistication and the decrease in youth violence may not seem so significant if it were not for the fact that many of the best-selling realistic video games contain graphic brutality and bloodshed. Popular opinion has targeted these games as inciting aggression and hostility in young players.

Among the types of video games that are most disparaged by concerned critics, parents groups, and some psychologists are "first-person shooters," in which the camera-eye of the video game player simulates the perspective of the protagonist in the video game world and the character/player is required to engage in a lot of combat to fulfill the mission of the game. Critics of this gaming category charge that the main character's realistic use of weapons and hand-to-hand combat skills desensitize players to violence and that the resulting fictionalized carnage is celebrated (even rewarded), leaving players ignorant of the real-world consequences and moral implications of such heinous actions. Illinois governor Rod Blagojevich has been at the forefront of recent efforts to keep minors away from such games. Worrying that first-person shooters involve players in the perpetration of violence (even if fictionalized), he remarked to reporters in 2005, "[Kids are] not spectators.

. . . They're the ones who cut people's heads off." Mary Ann Topping, a PTA president at Springman Middle School in Illinois who supported Blagojevich's push for a state law to forbid the sale of violent video games to minors, contended, "Since children are extremely impressionable and their brains are literally developing, violent games can and do have a hugely negative effect on them."

In December 2005, a federal judge struck down the law that Blagojevich eventually orchestrated, ruling that it was unconstitutional because it interfered with the right to free speech. Judge Matthew Kennelly asserted that in the United States the family, not the state, was responsible for limiting "protected speech." In his court opinion, Kennelly stated, "When the state defends a regulation of speech as a means to 'prevent anticipated harms' . . . it must do more than simply 'posit the existence of the disease sought to be cured.'" Instead, "[I]t must demonstrate that the recited harms are real, not merely conjectural, and that the regulation will in fact alleviate these harms in a direct and material way." In other words, as Ken Fisher, writing for the Web site *Ars Technica*, interpreted the ruling, "The mantra of 'games make kids violent' wasn't automatically true merely because it has been continually repeated in recent years, and the scientific evidence trotted out was unconvincing." A contemporary study conducted in part by the University of Illinois also found no evidence that playing violent video games was linked to increased player aggression. Professor Dmitri Williams, co-director of the study, told the university's news bureau that researchers have been quick to assume that violence in video games promotes hostility among players, "but, with the exception of relatively short-term effects on young adults and children, they have yet to demonstrate this link."

Some champions of video games argue that, instead of instructing children in the art of killing, even the most violent types of games teach skills that children need to know. For example, in a 2003 article for *Wired* magazine, James Paul Gee, the author of *What Video Games Have to Teach Us about Learning and Literacy*, claims:

> The phenomenon of the videogame as an agent of mental training is largely unstudied; more often, games are denigrated for being violent or they're just plain ignored. They shouldn't be. Young gamers today aren't training to be gun-toting carjackers. They're learning how to learn.

Gee insists that video games (including those with a lot of fighting) rely heavily on problem solving to see the main storyline to its conclusion. He maintains that first-person shooters stimulate role-playing and teach children how to order complex tasks to reach specific goals. He further suggests that these games are structured to test a player's skill level so that he or she will continue to play at their maximum degree of competency to overcome each new level of difficulty.

Many of these skills—problem solving, analytical thinking, multitasking—are just what future employers are looking for, and some educators are responding by incorporating video games into structured classroom activities. Avoiding games that involve violence, schools are experimenting with various video games that require resource management, monetary transactions, reading skills, and individual initiative to inspire student interest and test proficiency. Educators at the University of Rochester in New York who studied how video game play impacted visual skills concluded that players were capable of discerning large amounts of information from game screens. In a report for the *Science News for Kids* Web site, Daphne Bavelier, a neuroscientist at the university, stated, "Our findings are surprising because they show that the learning induced by video game playing occurs quite fast and generalizes outside the gaming experience."

Creative expression is also an element of video games that proponents number among the benefits of game play. In many games both violent and nonviolent, players can modify characters or units to suit their own tastes or even lay out whole cities based upon personal design choices. Emphasizing the role-playing nature of many video games (again, including first-person shooters), some commentators suggest that the creative choices implicit in these games can be connected to moral lessons. For example, some games such as the popular Xbox game *Fable* are designed to allow players to develop characters who are good, evil, or somewhere in between and follow specifically tailored storylines that reveal the consequences of making that moral choice. In an essay on popular myths about video games, Massachusetts Institute of Technology professor Henry Jenkins claims that games are a form of meaningful expression. He writes, "Many current games are designed to be ethical testing grounds. They allow players to navigate an expansive and open-ended world, make their own choices and witness their consequences." He then adds,

> [Popular role-playing game] *The Sims* designer Will Wright argues that games are perhaps the only medium that allows us to experience guilt over the actions of fictional characters. In a movie, one can always pull back and condemn the character or the artist when they cross certain social boundaries. But in playing a game, we choose what happens to the characters.

Thus, according to Jenkins and Wright, many role-playing video games allow the freedom to experiment with moral choices, including the use of violence and unwarranted cruelty, but do not let characters escape the consequences of those choices. Those who are skeptical of such claims, however, argue that any moral ramifications are locked within the game and have no impact on players who may adopt aggressive or sadistic game tactics in order to revel in the vicarious bloodshed.

In *At Issue: Video Games*, several authors address the emotional and psychological impact of video games upon young players. Some decry the amount of violence and adult content in popular games, while others extol the creative elements of what is designed to be an entertainment media. Still other critics and commentators in this anthology examine related controversies concerning video game content and its relation to social conventions and a changing, technology-centered culture. *Christian Science Monitor* staff writer Gloria Goodale asserts that "interactive entertainment is changing the way an entire generation sees itself in relation to the world." Therefore, the debates surrounding the personal and social impact of video games will likely continue as these games become more intricate, interactive, and entertaining.

1

Excessive Video Game Playing Can Adversely Affect Children's Health

Earl Hunsinger

Earl Hunsinger is a frequent contributor to Buzzle.com, an on-line news and information site. He has written on topics such as gardening, health issues, and computers.

Video games can negatively affect physical health and may also induce anti-social behavior in young people. Excessive video game playing encourages a sedentary lifestyle that can contribute to high blood pressure and obesity. When children spend up to twenty hours a week in front of video screens, they are foregoing exercise and outdoor play. Studies show that even brain development may suffer because playing video games involves little cerebral stimulation.

There have been literally thousands of studies done on whether the simulated violence in today's video games has a harmful effect on players. Most of these have recognized that there is a link between video game violence and antisocial behavior, especially in younger players.

For example, in the *Reader's Digest* article "Computer Violence: Are Your Kids at Risk?" Rick Dyer, a video game developer himself and the president of Virtual Image Productions, made the statement: "These are not just games anymore. These are learning machines. We're teaching kids in the most incred-

Earl Hunsinger, "Video Games and Your Child's Health," *Buzzle.com*, February 26, 2007. Reproduced by permission.

ible manner what it's like to pull the trigger. The focus is on the thrill, enjoyment and reward. What they're not learning are the real-life consequences."

Brent Stafford, a researcher at Simon Fraser University in British Columbia, Canada conducted a study involving 600 young video-game players. As a result, he warns that many games "are training our kids to celebrate violence." *Maclean's* magazine reports: "Some hard-core players who prefer the most violent and realistic games 'kill' as many as 1,000 'avatars' (on-screen characters) in a single night, often in scenes of gory realism." This research also showed the extent to which such violent games "engulf young minds in worlds that desensitize them to violence, even killing."

There was even a controversy recently [as of February 2007] over the online game, "Super Columbine Massacre RPG [role-playing game]," which allows players to act out the tragic events that took place at Columbine High School in Littleton, Colorado.

Non-violent Games Can Also Affect Health

Of course, not all computer or video games sponsor violence. Many are educational or encourage creative problem solving, such as the Myst series of games. However, even if a video game is not encouraging your children to go out and commit murder, there seems to also be concern about the effect that playing video games can have on a player's physical health.

Both [television and video games] have been accused of stifling creativity and the development of imagination.

For example, according to a study in Japan, computer games only stimulate a limited part of a child's brain. The study was done by Ryuta Kawashima, a professor at Tohoku University. It involved imaging the brains of children playing video games and comparing these images to those of children adding single digit numbers. The results showed that the children playing the video games used a smaller portion of their brains. Kawashima argued that if this was true for such a monotonous task as adding numbers, there would be an even greater difference compared to more complex activities, such as reading, playing outside, and interacting socially with others. Of course, the video game industry disagrees with this interpretation, arguing that various studies have shown that the moderate use of such games may actually be a positive experience. Even if moderation is the key, it doesn't seem to be the norm.

According to MediaWise "the average Everquest player, or EQer, plays twenty hours a week." Fans of other games devote similar amounts of time each week to video gaming.

In the U.S. about 40 percent of children between 5 and 8 years of age are considered to be clinically obese.

In addition to possible problems with brain development, Antonio González Hermosillo, president of the Mexican Society of Cardiology, stated in the *El Universal* newspaper of Mexico City that up to 40 percent of children who constantly play video games will develop high blood pressure. In addition to lack of exercise, this problem may arise because of the stress experienced by the players as they immerse themselves in situations that are perceived as dangerous, such as attacks, virtual fights, and other conflicts. The newspaper reported that he "warned that this will make cases of cardiovascular disease, the primary cause of death in Mexico, shoot up in the country."

Finally, we have to consider the similarities between video games and that other modern day impediment to going outside and playing, television. Both have been accused of stifling creativity and the development of imagination because they hand a story to the user, rather than forcing him or her to imagine it for themselves.

Video Gaming Causes Obesity

A more immediate, and more obvious, concern is the link between the use of these modern forms of entertainment and obesity. This link has nothing to do with the content of the game or television program, but rather with the time spent in these sedentary activities. The result is a lack of sufficient exercise. How bad is this problem?

It has been reported that in the U.S. about 40 percent of children between 5 and 8 years of age are considered to be clinically obese.

In 1996, Dr. Philip Harvey, a public-health nutritionist, was quoted in the newspaper *The Weekend Australian* as saying that "Australian children are getting fatter and they're getting fatter fast." His concern was based on a study that showed that the percentage of overweight children in Australia had doubled over the previous ten years. Every indication was that it was continuing to increase. The newspaper noted that just as with adults, lack of exercise was seen as the primary cause for this increase in obese children, with high-fat diets also a factor.

In 1993, Dr. Oded Bar-Or, a director of children's nutrition at Chedoke-McMaster Hospitals in Hamilton, Canada told *The Toronto Star*: "Today's children are fatter and more sedentary than ever before. Obesity among children has increased quite dramatically in the last 20 years." According to the *Star*, doctors have already "identified lack of exercise as a risk factor for . . . coronary heart disease, high blood pressure, diabetes and osteoporosis." Dr. Bar-Or concludes that "an inactive child is likely to be an obese adult."

In 1999 *The Sunday Times* of Britain quoted researchers as saying that one group of children they evaluated were "so inactive that their heart rates are little different awake from when they are asleep."

Finally, in 2000 Dr. Chwang Leh-chii, head of the dietitians' association of Taipei, Taiwan gave this warning, as reported in *Asiaweek*: "Obesity is one of the most serious health problems facing the youth of Asia." A study in Beijing showed that over 20 percent of primary- and secondary-school students there were overweight. Why? Because, according to the report, these Asian youths were spending more and more time watching TV and playing video games. *Asiaweek* went on to say that without a change in habits, including of course a more healthy diet, such overweight children could be facing high blood pressure, liver trouble, diabetes, and psychological problems.

Brent Stafford, quoted earlier, stated that the video-game industry, at $17 billion a year, is "bigger than film and television combined." Because of this, there is a good chance that your kids are already playing video games. The question is: Do you know what games they are playing, and for how long? More importantly: Do you know the impact that they may be having on your child's mental, emotional, and even physical health?

2

Some Video Game Playing Can Have a Positive Effect on Children's Health

Charlene O'Hanlon

Charlene O'Hanlon is a freelance writer based in New York. She is the editor and publisher of ACM Queue, *an online magazine for computer professionals.*

In 2004, West Virginia added the video game Dance Dance Revolution (DDR) to its middle-school physical education curriculum. The interactive game targets students' coordination, stamina, and balance and raises their confidence in gym class. Video games such as DDR not only provide healthy aerobic activity for kids, they also boost brain power. Kids who participate in physical activity during the school day show an increase in concentration and in their ability to learn. About 200 schools in the United States have since embraced video game playing in the classroom as well as the gymnasium.

The daily recipe for students' health and fitness is taking on a new ingredient long thought to be a poison: video games.

Plagued by one of the most overweight populaces in the country, the state of West Virginia was looking for a solution to its obesity problem that would appeal to the school-age crowd. It turned to Linda Carson, a professor at West Virginia University's School of Physical Education. Carson recalled wit-

Charlene O'Hanlon, "Gaming: Eat Breakfast, Drink Milk, Play Xbox," *T H E Journal*, vol. 34, no. 4, April 2007, pp. 34–39. www.thejournal.com/articles/20467. Copyright © 2007 T.H.E. Journal, LLC. 1105 Media Inc. Reproduced by permission.

nessing kids lining up in an arcade to play a fiercely kinetic video game called Dance Dance Revolution [DDR] and she suggested it as a possible remedy. So in the spring of 2004, the state partnered with the university on a research project to measure the effectiveness of DDR on combating childhood obesity.

In most circles, academic or otherwise, this would have seemed a most illogical, even goofy notion. According to popular wisdom, looking to a video game to correct weight gain makes as much sense as eating licorice to protect against tooth decay.

But Dance Dance Revolution doesn't jibe with popular wisdom. It isn't the sedentary, brain cell-gobbling narcotic generally associated with computer games. Its touchstones are coordination, stamina, and balance. DDR, which comes in versions for Xbox and PlayStation (and soon for the Wii), features a video screen and dance mat with nine tiles that light up to a driving dance beat. The object is to step on the tiles as they light up, while watching for clues in the form of arrows that flash all over the screen.

"Dance Dance Revolution sustains the kids because of the nature of the game," says Nidia Henderson, health promotions director of West Virginia's Public Employees Insurance Agency. "It's challenging, it's high-tech, it's easily accessible." And, above all, it's aerobic. Kids who would normally avoid regular exercise gravitate to DDR's light and sound.

Dance Dance Revolution Is a Hit at School

The state started with a clinical, at-home study of 50 children—all of whom had a body mass index above the 85th percentile, which is the threshold for being considered overweight. The initial results of the study were overwhelming. Pre- and post-testing showed, among other things, better arterial response to increased blood flow, an increase in aerobic capacity, and no weight gain. In addition, all the participants were more willing to try new activities and invite friends over to play, and were more confident in participating in physical education classes.

After seeing the data, West Virginia's department of education got involved and decided to implement a pilot program on 20 middle school campuses in the fall of 2004 to gauge DDR's acceptance within the general student population. The results of the pilot were similarly compelling.

So impressed was the state that it mandated Dance Dance Revolution be integrated in the physical education programs of all of its middle and junior high schools, with plans to expand it into the high schools and eventually the elementary schools. The state's gym teachers now are trained in how to use DDR and how to work it into a PE curriculum. Some schools are allowing children to play the game before and after school as a supplemental activity, and it's also being incorporated into school dances.

The mind-body connection has been heralded since ancient Greece.

Henderson says that West Virginia regularly consults with other states looking to follow its lead and implement the program. "The states are all very interested, but they face the same issue we do, which is funding," she says. "The industrial-strength dance mats are expensive." Fortunately, for West Virginia schools, the pilot garnered attention from Konami Digital Entertainment, the creator of DDR, which is now supporting the program with a $75,000 grant.

Physical Activity Helps Kids Learn

The incorporation of video games into physical education curriculum is an outgrowth of the larger trend of using gaming as a learning tool. While plenty has been written about the cognitive benefits of sedentary computer games, the positive effects of "movement" games such as Dance Dance Revolution are now making themselves known—and those effects go beyond physical fitness.

A study by the California Department of Education found that students who did just 10 minutes of rhythmic aerobics before a standardized test performed up to 25 percent better on the test than students who received 20 minutes of test-specific tutoring. And a recent research article by the National Institute for Health Care Management Foundation reported that breaks for physical activity during the school day can help children to be more focused and better able to learn.

Of course, this is not a new discovery. The mind-body connection has been heralded since ancient Greece. What's new is that schools are recognizing the link and are turning to video gaming, long considered anathema to both physical and mental vigor, to manifest it. "Most people think of games as dangerous, but if you put good stuff in them, they teach good stuff," says Debra Lieberman, a researcher in the Institute for Social, Behavioral, and Economic Research at the University of California-Santa Barbara, and a lecturer in the communication department.

Lieberman has done extensive research in the field of educational gaming and has developed a series of health-related video games that address diabetes, smoking prevention, and asthma. The games were created for the Nintendo gaming platform and distributed free of charge to drug companies and doctors' offices, which then passed them on to their patients.

"We wanted to develop confidence in children's ability to take care of themselves and then develop good health-behavior changes," Lieberman says. "The games were not responsible for teaching kids about the disease and how to deal with it—they already knew that. The games removed the stigmas of the conditions and helped reinforce and boost communication about them. It increased the social support for the kids."

That psychological boost seemed to translate into profound physical benefits. Lieberman and her team of researchers found in clinical trials that the asthma game, for example, reduced urgent care visits by 40 percent among the 200 asthmatic children it tested, and it decreased the number of missed school days. The diabetes game resulted in a 77 percent drop in doctor visits among its school-age participants (outpatients of diabetes clinics at Stanford University Medical Center and at a Kaiser Permanente clinic), from an average of 2.5 to 0.5 visits per year, she says.

"It was learning by doing, which works well," Lieberman says, "especially if the game is highly interactive."

Good gaming helps convince kids of their academic potential.

Getting FIT

About 20 schools across the country have signed up with Generation FIT (Fitness, Integration, and Training), a soup-to-nuts program designed to infuse daily exercise into curriculum and counter the de-emphasizing of gym class due to budget cuts. Generation FIT uses a video dance game in the style of Dance Dance Revolution called In the Groove, as well as other interactive video games such as Guitar Hero and Tetris. To play Guitar Hero, students stand on an elevated pad and mimic the movements of a guitarist on a video screen. The game helps improve hand-eye coordination and balance—it's not easy to stay on that pad. And this Tetris is not the familiar falling-blocks handheld unit; this game is played on the same mat used for In the Groove, and the students physically move the blocks around the mat. In addition to promoting physical fitness, the program 'encourages team building, leadership, and social interaction, and it intends to boost students' self-esteem, according to program creator Judy Shasek, a veteran in education and fitness program development.

The idea behind Generation FIT is to incorporate gaming into the classroom setting, in an unpopulated area of the room, to allow kids to get up and play the games at different intervals to keep their minds focused and re-energize them throughout the school day. Schools use the games in a number of different situations, as a replacement for a traditional gym program, or simply as a reward for students getting their work done early and correctly or for having overcome a hurdle.

Shasek calls her program "learning through fitness. We train one-third of the class to be leaders and manage the use of the fitness products. Students are empowered to see the difference in their lives, and changes in academic areas begin to happen."

Often the students chosen as leaders are those most in need of honing their social skills, Shasek says. She tells of one boy who rarely attended school, "and when he did go, he would always sleep. He was tattooed, pierced, looked different from the other kids, and was just so angry all the time. When the program was introduced at his school, he didn't want anything to do with the dance mats. I knew that Guitar Hero helps students with ADD and ADHD and those with balance problems, because of the special pad they have to stand on, so I convinced the teacher to put this boy in charge of Guitar Hero."

The teacher says the move paid off instantly. "That got him coming to class," says Julie Mann, an instructor at Success Academy, a small learning community in Redmond, OR. "He really enjoyed the game and was very proactive in getting it set up. There was an immediate change."

In Mann's experience, good gaming helps convince kids their academic potential. "They think they can't do it. Then they use the games and you can see them building their confidence in knowing they can do it. And that transfers into the classroom setting. I see it as a psychological thing—'Yes, you can do this. And you can do these other things, also.'"

"Once the next generation of instructors retires, this type of teaching and learning will be the norm."

According to Shasek, schools that have implemented Generation FIT report an overall increase in student participation, a drop in absenteeism, and a positive change in general attitude, as well as an increase in motor skills and coordination.

"We are always trying to manage fitness and learning," Shasek says. "When the body-brain [connection] is out of balance because of poor nutrition and lack of physical activity, students aren't in a good learning state—their retrieval and retention of memory is poor. Interactive gaming makes a huge difference."

The Name of the Game

Although incorporating gaming into curriculum is still considered avant garde to some, the argument against it is starting to lose relevance. As technology evolves, and games take on more sophistication and tap in to so many skill sets—and the positive research piles up—the scales are leaning so far in gaming's favor that naysayers are beginning to seem simply out of touch, or just plain stubborn.

Susan Haydock, gifted and talented consultant at the School District of Random Lake (WI), believes that eliciting greater acceptance of gaming from educators and parents may simply be a matter of changing the term itself, which lacks seriousness.

"I think it should be called a 'virtual learning environment,' not gaming," she says. "Because this is presented as gaming, people have a visualization—a preconceived notion—of what that is. And there are some forms of games that are like tabloids, and some that are really educational. But I think 'gaming' is a word that has had its time and place.

"I think we are in an evolutionary process," she adds. "Once the next generation of instructors retires, this type of teaching and learning will be the norm. Look at how life has changed with computers—shopping changed; learning at the adult level changed. The next step will be learning at the other levels."

Haydock worked with students on the River City Project, a simulation gaming environment that asks players to solve a growing health crisis among the residents of a virtual town. The game puts heavy emphasis on math and science principles, and draws on project management and collaboration skills. Haydock quickly noticed a difference in the thinking process of the participating students. "The students became very innovative. They were problem-solving at a very high level."

Kate Messner, a seventh-grade English instructor at Stafford Middle School in Plattsburgh, NY, whose students participated in the River City Project, believes the game actually plays to the current generation's strength at multitasking.

"One thing I found surprising was how easily the students adapted to the [game's] complexity," she says. "When I first previewed River City and saw all the different components . . . I thought it was a little overwhelming. Not so for the kids. They're a generation of multitaskers. They do their homework in front of the computer at night with a list of MP3s in one window, an essay in a second window, and two online chats happening in another one. For them, it's no problem to conduct research, interview residents, chat with their own teammates, and keep an eye on water samples all at the same time. It lets them learn in many different ways.

"If you think about it, every new thing had the fear of God put into it at first—comic books, radio, television, movies, music. This is just something that people are slowly getting used to."

3

Video Games Can Provide Health Benefits to the Sick

Betsy Streisand

Betsy Streisand is a senior writer at U.S. News & World Report.

New evidence suggests that video game playing can help heal sick and traumatized patients. Health professionals are prescribing video games to manage pain, chronic diseases, and even post-traumatic stress disorder. Video game companies, such as HopeLab in Palo Alto, California, are creating games geared specifically for patients' different needs. These games help educate the sick and focus on improving their health. Such innovations are getting positive results. For example, studies show that cancer patients who play video games are more likely to take their medicine and maintain higher levels of beneficial chemotherapy drugs in their blood than non-game-playing patients.

A teenager with Hodgkin's lymphoma blasts away at cancer cells in a computer game, all the while learning to do a better job of conquering her own cancer. A traumatized soldier returns to the cyber-generated streets of Iraq, in the hopes that he may be able to one day cope with the horrors of war. A young boy with severe burns delves into a virtual wonderland of snowmen, penguins, and snowballs, escaping, if only for a little while, the unbearable pain of having his wounds cleaned and dressed twice a day.

Welcome to the upside of computer games. Their legendary powers of distraction and ability to create synthetic worlds

Betsy Streisand, "Not Just Child's Play," *U.S. News & World Report*, vol. 141, no. 6, August 14, 2006, pp. 48–50. http://health.usnews.com/usnews/health/articles/060806/14video.htm. Copyright © 2006 U.S. News and World Report, L.P. All rights reserved. Reprinted with permission.

are turning one of the most popular—and disparaged—entertainment media into a promising and potentially powerful medical tool. Long derided as the enemy of health for transforming children into weapon-loving, overweight zombies, computer games are now proving effective for everything from reducing pain and managing chronic disease to treating post-traumatic stress disorder [PTSD] and promoting fitness and exercise. Although these so-called serious games are still in their infancy, there's a growing body of evidence backing their health-improvement claims. "Games can be extremely motivational and useful in therapeutic and medical settings," says Albert "Skip" Rizzo, a clinical psychologist and director of the Virtual Environments Lab at the University of Southern California. "There are a lot of researchers looking at this technology because it makes things fun, and it's very engaging."

Video Games Can Improve Health

Take that. Anyone who doubts this characterization need only attempt to come between a child and a Game Boy. Yet marshal that same hyperfocus in the service of, say, reducing pain, and it becomes a virtue, in Re-Mission, for instance, a new computer game for young cancer patients, the Tomb Raider-ish Roxxi leads players on a biological journey through the body. The patients zap cancer and infectious cells with chemotherapy and antibiotics, reinforcing the importance of keeping up treatment. The game is the brainchild of HopeLab in Palo Alto, Calif., a nonprofit founded by Pamela Omidyar (the wife of eBay founder Pierre Omidyar) that focuses on improving the health and quality of life of young people with chronic illnesses. Users say Re-Mission is as fun and challenging as popular commercial games. But it was designed to educate kids about cancer and its side effects and motivate them to stick with their treatments and promptly report symptoms. "It's hard to fight a teenager when they won't take their medicine," says Janet Franklin, an oncologist and clinical director of the Leukemia Lymphoma Program at Children's Hospital Los Angeles. "Video games draw teenagers in in a way we can't do with conferences and pamphlets."

Take Monzerratt Patino, 15, who has been playing Re-Mission since she was diagnosed with Hodgkin's lymphoma two years ago. "Before I played the game, I didn't really know how sick I could get if I didn't take my medicine," says Patino, who lives in Los Angeles. "The game explained how my white cells get affected by things and what happens to me," she says. "It was cool!"

There is no clinical test for cool, but preliminary results from a yearlong study of 375 cancer patients ages 13 to 29 (including Patino) found that those who played Re-Mission opened their pill bottles 15 percent more often and had levels of chemotherapy drugs in their blood 20 percent higher than the nonplaying group. Players also said they had a greater sense of empowerment against their cancer. HopeLab distributes Re-Mission free and wants to develop comparable resources for sickle cell disease, depression, and autism. Similar games are under development by others. The National Institutes of Health, for instance, has funded creation of games including Hungry Red Planet and the forthcoming Escape From Diab, both aimed at preventing childhood obesity.

Ironically, one of the most promising uses for computer games, long demonized for fueling couch potatoism and childhood obesity, is fitness.

Video Games Can Manage Diabetes and Promote Fitness

In a different twist on the video craze, there is Glucoboy, a blood glucose monitor that can be attached to a Nintendo Game Boy. The more a player regularly tests his or her glucose level—and it stays within an acceptable range—the greater the rewards like access to special games. The games are seeded with information on managing diabetes, including tips on diet, exercise, and monitoring blood sugar. Now awaiting Food and Drug Administration approval, Glucoboy was invented by a man whose son routinely hid his glucose meter to avoid the finger prick. "Diabetes is 90 percent self-management," says Richard Bergenstal, an endocrinologist and executive director of the International Diabetes Center at Park Nicollett in St. Louis Park, Minn. "If video games can be crafted to reinforce or enhance self-management, that's worth exploring."

Ironically, one of the most promising uses for computer games, long demonized for fueling couch potatoism and childhood obesity, is fitness. Health messages are easy to embed in games, and the new generation of computer cameras such as Sony's EyeToy, which projects the user's image on the screen, prompts youngsters to work up a sweat. The fitness benefits of playing Dance Dance Revolution, the hugely popular interactive video game in which players repeat a dance sequence and compete against each other online, have been well documented. Now that concept is being taken further at places like XRtainment Zone, a budding chain of video-fitness centers where the games are simulated but the workouts, from throwing a baseball to running in place to riding a bike, are real. The same concept is being used in rehabilitation, particularly for stroke victims, where the tedium of repeated motion exercises like reaching and bending often impedes progress.

Virtual Reality Helps Patients Escape from Pain

Going the standard video game one step further is virtual reality, where users wear goggles and enter a computer-generated universe that is so distracting it can actually ease pain and anxiety. "Virtual environments are so all-consuming that the deeper someone is absorbed into the game, the less they can focus on their own pain," says Hunter Hoffman, director of the Virtual Reality Analgesia Research Center at the University of Washington and the cocreator of SnowWorld, a virtual reality game for burn patients. SnowWorld takes players into an icy realm of penguins, igloos, and snowmen; users negotiate the terrain and engage in snowball fights. In a study now under review by the *Clinical Journal of Pain*, burn patients who played SnowWorld reported significantly lower levels of perceived pain during wound care: moderate or 5.1 on a scale of 10, compared with 7.2 or severe for those who did not play. A previous study found that the parts of the brain that register pain were less active while patients resided in the virtual world.

Heidi Neisinger didn't need a study to convince her of the value of an alternate universe. In 2003, her son pulled a pot of boiling water onto himself and spent months in excruciating recovery at Harborview Burn Center in Seattle. With burns over more than 30 percent of his body and his skin raw from graft sites on an additional 50 percent, Nathan, now [in 2006] 8 years old, got hysterical at the thought of his twice-daily treatments in the scrub tank, where his wounds were washed and dead skin removed. He was too young to safely be given enough narcotics to ease his pain. But when Nathan was playing SnowWorld, he was so completely transported that the nurses could lift his arms, stretch his skin, and clean him, sometimes without his noticing. "It was an ordeal every day," says Neisinger. "That game was an answer to my prayers."

Exposure Therapy Can Return Soldiers to Combat

Set the scene. If SnowWorld is meant to ignore a painful reality, the virtual worlds created to treat PTSD and phobias, for example, do just the opposite. Exposure therapy has long been the accepted method of treating PTSD, but it has an unavoidable flaw: Victims must re-create their trauma. "You never know exactly what they're imagining," says Rizzo, who has been using virtual reality to help soldiers returning from Iraq suffering from PTSD. "With VR we know what we're introducing into the scene."

Using a combat helmet equipped with VR goggles, a "base shaker" at foot level that vibrates to simulate riding in a humvee or tank, and a special machine to create smells such as burning gasoline, Rizzo can slowly return patients to combat. He can add, for example, familiar-looking buildings, the sounds of morning prayers, or a suspicious-looking merchant. He can also monitor a patient's emotional state. "If it gets to be too much, we back them out," says Rizzo, whose program is one of several being tested at military bases. VR is also being used to battle anxiety and phobias such as claustrophobia, which results in up to 20 percent of all MRIs being aborted midway by patients.

But VR can be expensive and has only recently [as of 2006] begun undergoing the type of clinical testing that would make doctors and insurers take notice. The interactive headset for SnowWorld, for instance, runs about $30,000. However, with more game makers and researchers focusing on video therapies, the cost and technology gap is expected to narrow.

It seems the perennially vilified video game may be on its way to a new reality: a hero of health and medicine.

4

Video Games Can Benefit Classroom Education

Marco Visscher

Marco Visscher is the managing editor of Ode, *an independent monthly magazine about the people and ideas that are changing the world.*

Many teachers as of 2006 began using videos games as instructional devices in their classrooms. Challenging puzzle games such as Myst and resource management games such as SimCity teach creative problem solving and other worthwhile skills by forcing students to formulate, test, and revise hypotheses. Video games also reinforce self-confidence and compel children to focus attention on an activity. Used properly in the classroom, video games have the power to keep students engaged in learning. People may disagree about whether video games should replace textbook learning, but in a society that is becoming more and more digital, it is evident that video games are teaching skills that cannot be experienced in traditional textbooks.

The door closes with a squeak and a creak. Oh no! Is it locked? Let's check. . . . No, thank God, you can open it. . . . So now, another go at getting to the ladder. Maybe through this narrow hallway? . . . No, it's a dead end.

Fifteen children between the ages of 9 and 11 are staring at the computer screen, mesmerized, as the adventure game Myst III: Exile is played. In the middle of the group sits Tim Rylands, the most popular teacher at the small elementary

Marco Visscher, "Reading, Writing and Playing The Sims," *Ode,* vol. 36, September 2006. Copyright © 2007 Ode Magazine USA Inc. Reproduced by permission.

school Chew Magna, in the village of the same name near the English city of Bristol. Once more he manuevers his cordless mouse to guide the cursor along the dark walls of a hollow mountainside. Rylands then tells his students, "Okay, now write down which way we should go to get to the ladder. What do you come across? What do you experience on your journey?" The only sound heard is the furious scribbling of pens.

Rylands has found a way to make writing fun for kids. Myst is a beautifully designed series of computer games set on a mysterious deserted island that can be endlessly navigated. According to Rylands, the visually rich landscape inspires his students' creativity.

Young people should not be memorizing facts or spending long hours on multiple choice tests.

He can back up that claim with data. An average of 75 percent of English children between the ages of 9 and 11 reach so-called "level four literacy levels" in reading and writing (including spelling, grammar, vocabulary, etc.). At Chew Magna, that percentage stood at 77 in 2000, rising to 93 four years later after Rylands began using computers to help teach writing. Boys in particular, who normally score lower in these areas, have made tremendous progress. One hundred percent reach level four, compared to 67 percent in 2000.

What Games Can Teach

Nolan Bushnell wishes his children had a teacher like Tim Rylands. "The digital life in which kids live today is turned off at school. That leaves them with boredom and frustration. A man in front of a blackboard with a piece of chalk is just very boring." Bushnell should know. He watched as his eight children became increasingly alienated in the U.S. educational system. He believes schools and teachers haven't sufficiently adjusted to changes in the world around them. Young people should not be memorizing facts or spending long hours on multiple-choice tests, says Bushnell, but learning to think, analyze, make connections. These are the talents that more than ever are rewarded in this new century, he says.

Bushnell also sees a solution for the educational system—the very idea Tim Rylands is already putting into practise: using video and computer games to inspire learning. He's an expert in the field. Back in 1972, Nolan Bushnell founded Atari, the pioneering computer company. As the creator of classics like Pong—remember the Ping-Pong game between two discs on opposite sides of the screen?—Bushnell is generally recognized as "the father of the game industry."

And because he is also the father of a 12-year-old son who can distinguish between 200 different Pokémon characters ("If they were plant and animal species, he would be able to pass sophomore biology"), Bushnell now spreads the word about how video games can help kids learn. Games, he asserts, teach you creative problem-solving. They teach you to formulate hypotheses ("First I have to get the key from the magician so I can open the door"), to test these hypotheses ("Game over") and revise them ("Oh no, I have to drink my elixir to get to the magician!"). Games can even teach you the fundamental principles of scientific research.

The number of games designed for educational or other purposes beyond play is a new, growing sector of the [video game] industry.

Back at Chew Magna school, Tim Rylands believes his students are learning more than writing skills. "While going through a game, children listen and talk," he explains as the classroom empties. "They discuss. They explore. It's like going on a school trip, but this is a lot cheaper, and it saves on insurance premiums," he jokes.

Many people envision that the school of the future—and Bushnell would love to open one himself—doesn't use books as its primary teaching materials, but video games. In the words of another game developer, Marc Prensky, who wrote *Digital Game-Based Learning*: "Because schools haven't adapted to the world their students know and live in, they simply get bored in the classroom. They tune out. You can get engagement, even among apathetic students, simply because games are constructed in a way so players want to finish the level. Games offer players the chance to make decisions, get feedback, level up and become heroes. That's how education should be organized. You learn more and more, you apply that knowledge, and you'll get a great job."

Game Developers Create Games for Schools

Computer games have already become part of the lesson plans in some schools. But these are usually simple games for elementary-school children. They use bright colours and amusing sounds to make math or spelling "fun." But these only take the edge off the age-old practise of rote learning. This is not the type of game-based education Bushnell and Prensky advocate.

Teachers like Tim Rylands (who won a teaching award last year from BECTA, the British government's partner in the development and delivery of its Internet-based learning strategy for schools, for his use of Myst) who have found ways to include exciting games in their teaching materials continue to be the exceptions. Some progressive secondary schools use SimCity (a simulation game in which you build cities) and Civilization (a strategy game that involves building a complete civilization). But supporters of the video-game industry—a $28 billion business in which annual sales in the U.S. now outstrip the Hollywood box office—see an opportunity to develop products tailored to schools. The number of games designed for educational or other purposes beyond play is a new, growing sector of the industry.

If video games inspire aggression, it is not reflected in the figures.

One example is a game recently developed by the United Nations called Food Force, in which young people learn about hunger issues by leading their own virtual food-aid campaign. It's now common in the corporate world to use computer and video games as part of refresher courses in numerous fields. And public-health officials are exploring the possibilities of games that encourage good health.

In *Got Game: How the Gamer Generation Is Reshaping Business Forever*, two organizational-development consultants explain that gamers are, in fact, ideal employees. They take more risks, react better to disappointments or mistakes, are open to the possibility that their plan may need to be adjusted and strive for excellence and promotions. Surprisingly, they also work better in teams—perhaps because of their experience working toward the same goal with others when they are playing computer games.

Most Bestselling Video Games Are Nonviolent

Many other people, of course, line up on the other side of the issue and their arguments are well known: The only thing kids learn from computer games is how to stare at a screen for hours. They're not using their brains and imaginations, just a few tendons in their fingers to operate the joystick. A salient detail: Most gamers are under the age of 40, while most critics are older and have rarely played the games themselves.

Parents are concerned that video games will make their children violent or uncommunicative. They get a lot of backing from vote-seeking politicians who voice their disgust with the violence and sexism seen in games. The media tend to focus on extreme examples like Grand Theft Auto, in which the player is a criminal who must survive by breaking into cars, robbing people and running over hapless pedestrians, and gets bonus points for killing cops. While arguably justified in such cases, the fear surrounding video games makes it difficult to look at the reality. The fact is that both youth crime and violent crime in Western countries has fallen spectacularly over the past 10 years as video-game popularity has risen. If video games inspire aggression, it is not reflected in the figures.

Moreover, the shooting games are not the most popular. Usually, only one or two violent titles rank among the top 10 bestselling games. The Progress & Freedom Foundation, a liberal think tank in Washington, calculated that over 80 percent of the most popular video and computer games of the past five years were rated "E" for everyone or "T" for "teen," i.e., they are not particularly violent.

There is also the concern that young people will become isolated by playing video games. But many games, particularly those played on the computer or the Internet, are designed for teams. Kid's social lives have changed a lot over the last 20 years, when few households had computers. Kids relied more on reading (certainly an isolating pursuit) and gamers were often lonely outsiders. But today, gaming is a very normal activity for most young people. In fact, nowadays a kid who's never played Nintendo or PlayStation is considered odd and often can't relate to others about an important leisure activity.

What is hard to grasp for those who aren't familiar with video games—people who grew up playing chess and Scrabble—that these new games invite creativity, promote problem-solving abilities and inspire perseverance. As Marc Prensky points out, it can take up to 100 hours to complete a video game: "This is not just biding time on a rainy day." Games stimulate the development of self-confidence and social contact with others. For people who have never experienced the sensation of reaching the final moment of the role-playing game Deus Ex (for which there are three possible endings!), these positive aspects are difficult to fathom—just as it's hard to understand what's so great about golf if you have never played it.

Games call on [kids'] natural need to develop themselves, to feel masterful and competent.

The bestselling computer game ever, The Sims, which has sold 6 million copies worldwide, is a simulation game (hence, The Sims) that allows you to control the lives of virtual characters. The Sims must spend enough time on education, physical activities, hygiene, eating and sleeping or they get sick. Players learn that you need to work to buy things, that you can earn more money if you spend time on personal development and social contacts and that you get depressed if your "pleasure meter" is empty. That's a far cry from a round of Parcheesi.

Games Encourage Students to Learn by Themselves

Games are interesting because they're difficult. That is the essential message the world of game culture offers to education: Learning is fun when it's intellectually stimulating. James Paul Gee, a professor of educational learning sciences at the University of Wisconsin as well as a fervent gamer and author of *What Video Games Have to Teach Us About Learning and Literacy*, explains it this way: "The game industry is selling products that are complex and hard to master, and take a lot of time to master. The fact that people are buying them contradicts the idea that everything should be fast and easy. In fact, a game that is too easy will get criticized in reviews and will not become a success. A game should be challenging, fair and deep. If it's not, it won't sell."

The insight that games are—in Ryland's words—"mind-expanding" rather than "mind-numbing" has not (yet) reached school curriculum developers. They continue to battle apathy among young people by trying to make teaching materials more fun and presenting them in bite-sized bits so they're easier to digest. It doesn't appear to be working. Kids are still bored in class. Teachers shake their heads, complain about the zap culture and the youth of today who can't keep their focus on anything, say that kids are quickly distracted and can't sit still. But if you put these bored kids in front of a PlayStation, they'll remain focused for hours. What happened to the short attention spans? Where's the apathy?

Video games support the great gift that young people possess to learn by themselves. Games call on their natural need to develop themselves, to feel masterful and competent. When they taste that thrill of possibility, it can bring feelings of pleasure and pride. Anyone who has played Legend of Zelda or Morrowind knows what it's like to complete the game at last after many lengthy periods of frustration.

In this context, video games present a radically different vision of education: kids who are able to learn by themselves. Even when schools fail, students actively look for ways to learn. Experts don't need to impose an education program to tap into that innate need.

Video Games Keep Students Engaged

Making History is a good example of a computer game especially developed for education that fulfils young people's requirements for quality and challenging entertainment. The game is used to teach the history of World War II. Even before our meeting in Boston, Nick deKanter, co-founder and vice president of Muzzy Lane Software, throws out a challenge. "Does the game simplify history? Why don't you play first and ask me later?" DeKanter is right. Making History: The Calm and the Storm sketches a simplified image of a particular moment in human history. During the game you take on the role of a head of state who leads his country based on historical events and data. You have to make decisions (on spending, trading partners, military strategies and much more) as well as conduct negotiations with other government leaders. Military, diplomatic and economic advisers are built into the game and prompt you at crucial moments. The instruction booklet is 58 pages long.

[G]ames should never be played in a vacuum, and they should never be used as a babysitter.

David McDivitt, a history teacher at Oak Hill High School in the U.S. state of Indiana, uses the game. His research shows that the students who didn't read textbooks or attend classes but played and discussed Making History learned more about World War II than students in other classes. Moreover, answers to essay questions in the classes exclusively using the game were more reflective and better reasoned.

But what most struck McDivitt was that his students talked about the game outside the classroom. "There were conversations about game scenarios spilling out in the hallways, the lunch room and even after school," he notes, "with some kids coming in after 3 wanting another turn! Once I heard someone say: 'Hey dude, you weren't supposed to invade my country, we had a defence agreement!' Extracurricular conversations about the politics of leadership are not something I typically see after reading a chapter of a textbook."

DeKanter agrees. "A textbook is much better than a video game at delivering names and dates," he explains. "But in today's world, data is available anywhere on the Internet. What's more important now than learning names and data are the skills to analyze that data and to apply information to gain insight and make decisions. In the Information Age it's all about connecting the dots—and games are, much more than books, extremely good at helping students learn this."

But he is also realistic. "People learn from other people, not from machines. That's why games should never be played in a vacuum, and they should never be used as a babysitter. A game needs to be introduced and evaluated. Have students write a paper on how they performed in the game and what they learned. I don't see games as a replacement for textbooks, but as a valuable enhancement."

Atari founder Nolan Bushnell disagrees. He would love to set up a private school at which children learn through games. Textbooks would not be used. "We don't need books," he says decidedly. "Sure, kids need to read, but not necessarily books. Books are obsolete." The restaurant chain he is currently developing as part of his new company uWink could be a good model for his school; there, small groups sit around tables playing stimulating games surrounded by walls onto which facts and data are projected.

[D]igital culture has society ever more firmly in its grasp.

But won't educational games always lose out to their commercial equivalents purely focused on entertainment? "That's not the competition here," Bushnell replies. "Educational games are competing against the boring teacher in the front of the class who is just not capable of engaging his students."

Even Socrates Would Have Approved of Video Games

The resistance to games shows all the signs of a ritual conflict between generations. At one time, rock 'n' roll was thought to have a clearly negative influence: Parents, preachers and politicians thought it changed young people into—according to one U.S. preacher—"devil worshippers" who defied both the law and common decency. Further back, jazz and even the waltz were criticized as corrupting influences, as were novels, comic books and movies—all said to dull the minds of young people. In retrospect, I think we can all agree those influences weren't so bad.

More to the point, we currently consider books a higher form of culture, but one of history's most eminent philosophers, Socrates, was a declared opponent of reading. Books would render people forgetful, he claimed. According to Plato's *Phaedrus*, Socrates believed you shouldn't even write down a speech because the written word always provides "one unvarying answer." This recently led *The Economist* to suggest that Socrates was criticizing books' lack of interactivity and that if alive today he might be a champion of video games.

It is evident that digital culture has society ever more firmly in its grasp. It is clear that computers and the Internet are creating endless new opportunities. And it is inevitable that this powerful cultural influence won't stop at the classroom door. Standard classroom teaching, from which Tim Rylands' students momentarily escape when Myst is played would appear to be better suited to a time when young people were being prepared to work in an economy based on factories and mass production. It doesn't take a lot of insight to recognize that the modern economy requires very different talents—talents that may not be fully developed using traditional textbooks. The advance of video games into classroom education, therefore, is not only unavoidable; it is necessary.

5

Video Games Can Shape Players' Beliefs

Matthew Quirk

Matthew Quirk is a staff editor at the Atlantic Monthly, *where he reports on education and other subjects.*

As the video game market has become a mainstream, multi-million-dollar industry, game designers and advertisers have begun to tap into the persuasive aspects of video games. Both the Republican and Democratic parties have created games that attempt to sway players' opinions in regard to political issues. Other game makers ask players to question their own beliefs about social issues such as abortion. Moreover, the more compelling and action-packed an issues-oriented video game is, the more likely its persuasive messages will be internalized by players. For instance, the popular game, America's Army, created originally as a recruiting tool for the Army, has attracted a loyal online following that now has a more positive opinion of the armed forces thanks to the structure and details of the game.

Is the surest way to our brains through our thumbs? Ian Bogost thinks so. As the head of Persuasive Games, a video-game design studio, he is the brain whom Democrats, Republicans, Best Buy, and even Jeep turn to when they want to plant a message in your head. And as a professor at the Georgia Institute of Technology, Bogost writes long books about how the beeps and blips on a screen are uniquely suited to

Matthew Quirk, "Fun and Friendly Persuasion," *National Journal*, vol. 38, no. 29, July 22, 2006, pp. 58–59. Copyright © 2007 by National Journal Group, Inc. All rights reserved. Reprinted with permission from National Journal.

jarring our most firmly held beliefs. To that end, he's got a 717-page manuscript that is now being pared down by MIT Press and a new video game that tackles the most intractable, deeply felt, incendiary issue in American public life: abortion.

It's an opportune time to be doing research into video games and building a business based on the premise that what you play can shape what you believe. Video games have become a mainstream medium on par with film (game revenues now exceed those of the box office) and radio (games are projected to outsell the music industry by 2008). More and more Americans get their politics interactively, online: Thirty-eight percent of broadband users cite the Web as their main source of political information. The last presidential election brought with it the first presidential campaign video game (for Howard Dean, designed by Bogost), and both major-party nominees eventually had their own games. Advertising inside games produced $56 million in revenue last year, and that number is projected to grow to $732 million by 2010. Half of the U.S. population plays video games.

Bogost says that games, with their set rules dictating what a player must do to win, are uniquely suited to interact with the beliefs and values that constrain our behavior in the real world. In his academic articles and books, laden with obtuse neo-Marxist theory, Bogost argues that game designers, by setting up those values in the virtual space of a game, can easily hold a player's beliefs up for "interrogation" and punch holes in them.

His commercial work is far more straightforward. His clients aren't interested in having their messages deconstructed. But in his campaign games, he uses the rules and reinforcements of video games to drive home the sponsor's point.

Take a video game he made for Republicans in the Illinois House called Take Back Illinois. It looks something like Sim-City—the groundbreaking video game that lets players act as politicians and urban planners in trying to manage a large city. In the Illinois game, you have to educate, care for, and gainfully employ the people of an entire state by setting policies and shooing residents to and from schools, hospitals, and jobs. As you play, you soon learn you can succeed only by hewing to Republican principles (if you don't cap damages in medical-malpractice lawsuits, for instance, doctors flee, hospitals close, and your little icon citizens start turning green and dying at a terrific clip).

When asked if he is brainwashing people with games like these, Bogost responds: "You're forced to understand the position to be successful. But you have the opportunity to immediately reject it."

[Persuasion games] are boring—at least compared with commercial hits.

Hundreds of video games are now devoted to news and politics. Any major controversy immediately spawns an interactive version (Bogost maintains a running list at watercoolergames.org). You can shoot illegal immigrants, massacre students at Columbine, run from the Janjaweed in Darfur, hunt with Dick Cheney, trade bullets with the Israeli Defense Forces, and so on. The vast majority of these games, however, merely paste some political images or context onto old action games.

Bogost embeds persuasion deep in the game itself. The principles being pushed needn't be presented up front or argued. By playing the game—frantically clicking away and trying to fend off failure—the player realizes, and eventually internalizes, which values work and which don't. Regardless of political stripe, everyone wants to win. To do so, you must accept the sponsor's basic cause-and-effect premises.

"A video game is very sneaky when it comes to persuasion," says B. J. Fogg, a Stanford University psychologist and behavioral scientist who studies how to persuade people digitally. (You have him to thank for the annoying pop-ups on your screen.) "Our minds have a difficult time distinguishing between reality and simulation, especially when you suspend disbelief and your mind is absorbed in making sense of the game."

Bogost is pursuing his idea that video games can lead to more free-thinking rather than less with his new game about abortion. No one gets an abortion in the game. Rather, a game engine—"an ideologically biased artificial intelligence"— teases out the player's attitude toward abortion in the early rounds and progressively, through a series of virtual experiences, forces the player to consider the opposing point of view without explicitly putting it across. An abortion-rights supporter would be routed through a set of experiences designed to underscore the sanctity of life—playing with an infant, for instant, or living in a world that depicts the loss of life after an abortion. An opponent of abortion rights, meanwhile, might find himself in a simulated household trying to budget time and money to support two children as a single parent holding a minimum-wage job. The only way to win is to move a certain distance away from your original beliefs.

[America's Army] seeks to instill the Army's values by deliberately forcing virtual recruits through the tedium of basic training.

However, even Bogost's most sophisticated games share a weakness common to the political genre. They're boring—at least compared with commercial hits. Nicco Mele was Howard Dean's Webmaster and worked with Bogost on the Dean game. Although the 2004 campaign games, Howard Dean for Iowa and the Republican National Committee's John Kerry: Tax Invaders, attracted lots of attention and players, he says, "both are still pretty amateur-hour." The political agenda was in the foreground, game play was in the back.

Mele, a friend of Bogost's, says that the natural home for persuasion games may not be in campaigns but in big-budget productions. These games are analogous to films like *Fahrenheit 9/11* and *The Passion of the Christ* because they merge the popular and the political. Indeed, a new crop of big-budget games is emerging, where the political message is hidden in a game so compelling that the designer can slip anything past our critical faculties. According to this theory, Fogg says, the more diverting the game, the more distracted the player, the lower the defenses, the more potent the propaganda.

Well-heeled sponsors outside of political campaigns are proving that it's a potent mix to combine the slow inculcation of values that Bogost describes with an addictive, big-budget game.

The Army initially spent more than $7 million on America's Army, its first-person shooter game, as a recruitment tool. But since its initial release in 2002, the game has been remarkably successful in turning public opinion as well. Rather than glamorize the Army, however, or indulge the run, shoot, kill approach of many first-person shooter games, the game seeks to instill the Army's values by deliberately forcing virtual recruits through the tedium of basic training. Even the sound effects are chosen scientifically to reinforce memorization. "Honor points" keep track of how closely a player cleaves to those values, and accumulating points is necessary to open up advanced features of the game. Run past a fallen soldier, and you lose points. Shoot a civilian, you may end up in a Fort Leavenworth prison. The game slowly drives home the point that the Army is a desirable way of life, and it keeps players going because of its high production values and addictive game play. And it works. Thirty percent of Americans ages 16 to 24, according to a marketing survey for the Pentagon, have a more positive impression of the Army because of the game, which has been continuously expanded.

Evangelical conservatives are also getting into the game market. Troy Lyndon, a Christian activist and developer of bestselling video game franchises such as Madden Football and Street Fighter, bought the rights to make a shoot-'em-up game called Left Behind: Eternal Forces based on the hugely successful Left Behind series of action novels about the Apocalypse. An evangelical message is woven into the game play. The Apocalypse just happened; you're in a still-smoking Lower Manhattan, part of a group of evangelicals who must convert or kill unbelievers and lukewarm Christians who are left on Earth. The moral—convert or be damned (maybe shot as well)—is also driven home in sermon-like exhortations between scenes. The player's success is determined in part by "spirit points," which reward prayer and obedience to the game's message.

Left Behind Games has a two-pronged marketing strategy. It will reach rapture-minded evangelicals by distributing 1 million sample games to churches. A second tactic plays down the overt Christian message and goes after mainstream audiences by extolling the quality of the game play and by citing reviews from mainstream critics.

Bogost hopes that every game carries with it the seeds of its own deconstruction and that games are inevitably a force for opening minds. But the medium is quickly becoming another well-financed, well-tuned instrument of persuasion, of a piece with the mass of other political messages that attempt to win, rather than inform, the debate.

Violent Video Games
Teach Anti-Social Behavior

Linda Piepenbrink

Linda Piepenbrink is a writer and editor at Maranatha Baptist Bible College, which publishes In Focus, *a magazine for Christian teenagers. She has written for such magazines as* Virtue, Christianity Today, *and* Today's Christian Woman.

Video games with graphic, violent content teach young players that violence is acceptable in society. These games cause aggressive behavior in viewers, distorting their worldview and making them more likely to defy authority figures such as the police or their parents. Human life is sacred, but violent video games suggest that it is okay to kill people. Repeated exposure to such games desensitizes people to violence and even stunts the development of the portion of the brain that controls decision making, learning, and moral judgment. Finally, playing violent video games draws a player's attention away from pursuing a virtuous life and a relationship with God.

Take two seconds and name your favorite video game or movie. Does it include any violence? If you're a typical American teen, by age 18 you've entertained yourself with 16,000 simulated murders and 200,000 acts of violence in movies, TV, and video games. In some homes, kids are banned from watching R-rated movies, but in their bedrooms and friends' homes, they spend countless hours in front of a video monitor killing people and mowing down pedestrians. Some

Linda Piepenbrink, "You Are What You Watch," *In Focus*, Fall 2005. www.mbbc.edu. Reproduced by permission.

video games even give bonus points for shooting people in the head. Just harmless entertainment, right? Consider a few facts:

Violent media messages teach you that violence is the accepted way to solve problems. When 18-year-old Devin Moore was arrested for stealing a car, he grabbed a pistol from the police officer and gunned down three officers in less than a minute. Before that, he had never been seen with a weapon. But for months before the shootings, he had spent time stealing cars and killing cops in Grand Theft Auto, the best-selling video game played by a majority of American teenage boys. A civil suit against Moore and the makers and retailers of the game is pending [as of 2005]. (Recently, the San Andreas version was changed from a "Mature" rating to a more restrictive "Adults Only" rating after an investigation showed that pornographic content could be unlocked on the game.)

The object of the most popular blockbuster video games is to kill people.

Media Violence Causes Aggressive Behavior

While graphically violent video games are not the only cause of real-life violence, playing violent videos will not make you a peaceful problem solver. More than 1,000 studies show a link between media violence and aggressive behavior in viewers. The American Academy of Pediatrics, the American Medical Association, and other watchdog groups agree that viewing repeated acts of violence desensitizes the brutality of violent behavior and can make you violent. One 17-year study concluded that "teens who watched more than one hour of TV a day were almost four times as likely as other teens to commit aggressive acts in adulthood." Don't assume you're the exception. Besides . . .

Violent entertainment can give you a bad attitude. Maybe you won't go on a killing spree, but prolonged exposure to murder and mayhem may influence you in other ways—distorting your view of the world, exposure causing you to argue more or lose your temper, to feel self-important, to defy authority, to abandon your parents' teaching, or to want immediate gratification. Wow. But that's not all.

Repeated exposure to violent entertainment does not please God.

Watching a steady diet of violence teaches you that human life is not sacred. Believe it or not, Atari once had a rule that "you could blow up a tank, a plane, a car—but you couldn't do violence against a human," says Atari creator Nolan Bushnell, who is bothered by the antisocial behavior promoted by today's video games. The object of the most popular blockbuster video games is to kill people—with blood and chunks of bodies flying in different directions. Eventually, those images become less shocking and result in a lack of empathy for human suffering and death.

Do Not Make Violence an Idol

Watching violence can stunt your brain. New research shows that because the brain is not fully developed until young adulthood, video game use may idle and impoverish the development of the pre-frontal cortex. the portion of the brain associated with decision making and behavior control, as well as the development of memory, moral judgment, and learning. MRI [magnetic resonance imaging] scans of teens playing violent video games showed decreased brain activity in the frontal lobe. And during violent scenes, emotional parts of the brain were shut down.

Repeated exposure to violent entertainment does not please God. Come on, does God really care whether we view violence as entertainment? After all, the Bible contains plenty of gory violence. Consider Jael who jammed a tent peg through her enemy's temple or Jezebel's blood spattering on the wall as she fell to the ground and was eaten by dogs. Yet, the Bible never glorifies violence or takes it lightly. Even the crucifixion of Christ is sparing in its details. It's highly unlikely that anyone would go on a shooting rampage after reading 1 and 2 Samuel too often. But Eric Harris and Dylan Klebold, who were addicted to Doom and other violent games, killed 12 classmates and a teacher, and wounded 24 other students before committing suicide at Columbine High School.

Their actions remind us that everyone has a sinful nature and a heart that is "deceitful above all things, and desperately wicked" (Jeremiah 17:9). Who can trust it? When the earth was "filled with violence," as recorded in Genesis 6, God was grieved and sent a worldwide flood to destroy everyone but righteous Noah and his family.

Repeated exposure to the Bible will teach you to discern. Although the Bible doesn't mention video games, it has plenty to say about violence, along with warnings and principles to help you make right choices. Consider a few: Proverbs 3:31 says, "Envy thou not the oppressor (violent man), and choose none of his ways." Psalm 140:4 could be applied to violent video games and those who make them: "Keep me, O Lord, from the hands of the wicked; preserve me from the violent man; who have purposed to overthrow my goings." Psalm 119:133 says, "Order my steps in thy word: and let not any iniquity have dominion over me." Psalm 101:3 says, "I will set no wicked thing before mine eyes." Galatians 5:19–26 warns Christians to put off the works of the flesh, such as "hatred," "strife," and "murders" and to put on "love, joy, peace," etc.

It's not enough to just get rid of the violence in a sort of reformation. If you realize you've wasted many hours in slavish indulgence to violent movies and video games, you should repent for making violence an idol and for allowing the seductive "wine of violence" to draw you away from a pure relationship with the Lord (Prov. 4:17). King Josiah was only 12 when he began to purge Judah of idolatry. For you, that may mean replacing that James Bond video game or violent movie with a more wholesome activity. Still unconvinced? Here's what God thinks: "The LORD trieth the righteous: but the wicked and him that loveth violence his soul hateth" (Ps. 11:5). Yet "whoso confesseth and forsaketh [his sins] shall have mercy" (Pr. 28:13).

See No Evil?

Seeing realistic depictions of violent acts is not always bad. For example, after the Jewish holocaust of nearly 6 million people was exposed, American school children were exposed to graphic photographs of the victims to show the reality of violence and to prevent the horror from being repeated. Similarly, prolife groups have stirred controversy by showing real photos of bloody aborted babies to expose the horror of abortion.

The purpose of such powerful depictions of violence is to prevent further violence, not to invite more murder. Ask yourself, Does the video or movie I am playing or watching have a redeeming purpose? Is it helping me to become more like Christ? Or is the violence just gratuitous? If, for example, your purpose is just to alleviate boredom or to practice eye-hand coordination, it's time to find something better to do.

7

Video Games Do Not Cause Violence

Rashawn Blanchard

Rashawn Blanchard writes on gaming, music, pop culture, and social issues for Associated Content, *an online news and information site that publishes original multimedia resources.*

Video games are unfairly targeted as the cause of violent behavior in young people. Many different forms of entertainment such as cartoons, reality television shows, and movies contain violence and have the power to influence people, yet these are not so vigorously held to account. Regardless, most game players can tell reality from fantasy and have a level of common sense that prevents them from emulating the violence in media. Instead, the violence in video games simply helps players find release from the frustrations in their daily lives.

After the tragic events that transpired at the Virginia Tech campus shooting [April 16, 2007] the effect of violent video games has once again been called into question. The same reaction to video games containing violent images and game play [arose] after the events of the Columbine shooting and many parents railed against what these games were doing to the youth of America. Entertainment shouldn't be sold short, as it does tend to influence people. However, when it truly comes down to it, it would be ludicrous to place the blame of violent, unforgivable actions upon a popular form of entertainment. If it were any bit true then the United States

Rashawn Blanchard, "Video Games and Violence: Not Causing Tragedies Since 1971," *Associated Content*, May 1, 2007. Reproduced by permission.

alone would have somewhere in the vicinity of a quarter of its population teetering on the edge of violent explosion from a few hours with Grand Theft Auto III.

Video games have long since been defined as a form of entertainment and it would be foolish not to acknowledge the fact that entertainment does influence people, especially children. In the 90's and even still to a degree today, elementary school children can be seen practicing their karate kicks even though they've had no martial arts training. This could be contributed to the amount of live-action costume super heroes that had taken over Saturday morning children's lineups, namely the Mighty Morphin' Power Rangers.

Years later, those influenced by television would turn to random acts of stupidity as the MTV show *Jackass* influenced legions of fans to perform their own random [stunts]. Many sent home videos to MTV and others were hurt, prompting MTV to show a warning before each episode of *Jackass* and spinoffs of the show. People have always attempted wrestling as it has been shown by the WWE(F) [World Wrestling Entertainment (formerly Federation)] and the former competition.

[T]he allure of some of the violence is to release frustrations that go on in the real world.

Game Players Have Common Sense

Even though these other forms of entertainment have been emulated by youngsters across the country none of them have come under the fire that video games have. Violence is commonplace in video games and complaining about the violence has led to the founding of the ESRB [Entertainment Software Rating Board].

While people choose to emulate certain video games such as fans of Street Fighter performing a motion that in-game would yield a fireball or Final Fantasy fans performing a motion that would yield a magical result, there is a level of common sense that intercedes before they pick up and proceed to beat a prostitute to death to get their money back while refilling their health meter as seen in Grand Theft Auto [GTA]. The level of absurdity that is seen in these games is something that gamers know they can't do in real life—that is one of the core reasons that many people play the game.

The popular God of War series is known for its brutal combat, where the gamer is rewarded for being as ruthless as possible. On the special features disc that is included with the second installment of the series, developers go on to mention that the allure of some of the violence is to release frustrations that go on in the real world. The entire idea of an escape from reality can be used to explain entertainment in general, of which video games are parts of.

Some Games Are More Violent than Others

What are routinely not mentioned by those who would seek to ban controversial violent games are their counterparts in the violent spectrum. Several action titles, usually military video games (such as Ghost Recon) seldom come under fire from those who attack Grand Theft Auto. The violence is not senseless but in many cases it is much more brutal. Air Strikes, artillery barrages, rockets and explosions all create a much more heinous aftermath than what can be found in one block of a GTA city.

The most important notion, however, is that as human beings (not as gamers) there is a distinct realization between video game violence and real life violence. People in general do not want to bring harm to one another for no reason and playing a video game simply isn't a large enough reason to force someone out of the comfort of their living room and onto a sidewalk with a shotgun and an aimless vendetta.

8

Video Games Are Unjustly Targeted by Anti-Violence Crusaders

Daniel Koffler

Daniel Koffler was the 2005 Burton C. Gray Memorial Intern for Reason *magazine. As a senior at Calhoun College at Yale University in 2006, he wrote a biweekly column on varied topics for the* Yale Daily News.

American politicians frequently target video games for increased legislative regulation over mature subject matter such as violence or sexually explicit content. However, their arguments that violent video games are negatively affecting American children are emotionally driven and are not supported by scientific research. With the wide range of media options available to everyone today, it does not make sense to target a very small percentage of video games for increased regulation, especially when the bills that the politicians draft against video gaming are routinely overturned in court.

In May [2005], by a vote of 106 to 6, the Illinois legislature passed a measure banning the sale of "violent" and "sexually explicit" video games to minors. The California Assembly is [as of October 2005] considering its own version of a prohibition on game sales to the under-aged, and Washington, Indiana, and Missouri already have enacted similar laws, only to see them struck down on First Amendment grounds.

Daniel Koffler, "Grand Theft Scapegoat," *Reason*, vol. 37, no. 5, October 2005, pp. 72–73. Copyright (c) 2005 by Reason Foundation, 3415 S. Sepulveda Blvd., Suite 400, Los Angeles, CA 90034, www.reason.com. Reproduced by permission.

Video games are an appealing target for a public figure in search of a crusade. Movies and music have energetic advocates, but it's hard to find anyone who will defend games for their artistic value, or even on the grounds of freedom of expression. Usually the strongest argument made for games is that they are harmless fun. That's not the most effective response when the governor of Illinois is claiming "too many of the video games marketed to our children teach them all of the wrong lessons and all of the wrong values"

Ominously, the Illinois proposal pays no heed to the existing range of voluntary content ratings, which run from EC ("Early Childhood") to AO ("Adults Only") and ostensibly allow game merchants to decide for themselves what constitutes "violent" or "sexually explicit" material. In a message "to the parents of Illinois" Democratic Gov. Rod Blagojevich asserts that "ninety-eight percent of the games considered suitable by the industry for teenagers contain graphic violence." Blagojevich is surely abusing language and statistics—if you stretch the phrase far enough, even the mild-mannered Super Mario Bros. includes what could be described as "graphic violence"—but the implication is that the proposed legislation's content restrictions could apply to games the ratings board approved for teens.

Emotional Appeals Drive Criticism Against Video Games

It would not be fair to say that the arguments for video game criminalization are completely uncontaminated by evidence. But prohibitionists are highly selective about the evidence they present and are careless once they've presented it, hoping to substitute raw emotional appeal for a plausible explanatory framework. Blagojevich, for example, claims "experts have found that exposure to violent video games increases aggressive thoughts, feelings, and behaviors"—as if no more need be said about the causal relationship between playing video games and engaging in anti-social behavior. Such rhetoric implies that video game players are empty, infinitely corruptible ciphers.

There is no shortage of readily available literature on the relationship between media exposure and behavior, and the evidence does not support the prohibitionists' case. A 2004 study of "Short-Term Psychological and Cardiovascular Effects on Habitual Players," conducted by researchers at the University of Bologna, concluded that "owning videogames does not in fact seem to have negative effects on aggressive human behavior." A 2004 report in the *Journal of the American Medical Association* noted: "If video games do increase violent tendencies outside the laboratory, the explosion of gaming over the past decade from $3.2 billion in sales in 1995 to $7 billion in 2003, according to industry figures, would suggest a parallel trend in youth violence. Instead, youth violence has been decreasing."

The sheer scope of media choices renders futile any effort to rein in content through regulation.

Likewise, criminologist Joanne Savage contends in a 2004 issue of *Aggression and Violent Behavior* that "there is little evidence in favor of focusing on media violence as a means of remedying our violent crime problem." In the absence of a wave of real-life, game-inspired carnage, Harvard Medical School psychiatry professor Cheryl Olson, writing in the journal *Academic Psychiatry* in the summer of 2004, advised that "it's time to move beyond blanket condemnations and frightening anecdotes and focus on developing targeted educational and policy interventions based on solid data."

Politicians Bludgeon Popular Culture

Unfortunately, blanket condemnations and frightening anecdotes are likely to be with us as long as they prove electorally profitable. In March [2005], Sens. Hillary Clinton (D-N.Y.), Joseph Lieberman (D-Conn.), Sam Brownback (R-Kan.), and Rick Santorum (R-Pa.) jointly proposed a $90 million appropriation to study the effects of games and other media on children. Apparently, no one on any of the senators' staffs could be bothered to point out that there already is plenty of credible research on precisely that question. Either that, or a bipartisan coalition of presidential aspirants calculated that bashing game designers could be a cheap way to endear themselves to family-values voters.

This is hardly the first time politicians have attempted to bludgeon popular culture into submission. (Recall the political grandstanding that followed past moral panics over movies, comic books, and rock music.) What separates efforts to curb children's exposure to video games from older, parallel campaigns is how profoundly out of touch they are with the realities of the entertainment choices available to children.

For example, Hillary Clinton—fresh from her collaboration with Santorum and Brownback, and consistent with her advertised principle of "fighting the culture of sex and violence in the media"—decided in mid-July [2005] to intervene in the controversy over the "Hot Coffee" mod for the game Grand Theft Auto: San Andreas. Hot Coffee is a hidden component of the game's coding that, if unlocked via a program that can be freely downloaded from the Internet, will treat a player to scenes of grainy, polygonal sex. Outraged Clinton wrote a letter to the Federal Trade Commission urging it to investigate whether Rockstar (the company that produces GTA) created the Hot Coffee content. She seemed oblivious to one of the first lessons a new Web surfer learns: There is a universe of free Internet pornography that anyone looking online for explicit sex can see without bothering to download and install a video game modification.

The sheer scope of media choices renders futile any effort to rein in content through regulations. Occasional pixelated displays of violence and sex can be found in some games that are sometimes sold to children. (Sixteen percent of games are rated "Mature," and 16 percent of game buyers are under 18, according to the Entertainment Software Association.) These comprise a tiny part of the total array of media content freely available to anyone.

Legislators nevertheless are drafting self-righteous bills that practically beg to be overturned in court. With any luck, that will keep the prohibitionists occupied until they discover the next dire threat to our children.

9

Popular Video Games Are Often Misogynistic

Lauren Sandler

Lauren Sandler is a freelance writer whose work has appeared in the Atlantic Monthly, *the* New York Times, *the* Los Angeles Times, *the* Nation, *and* Salon.com. *She has produced cultural features and news segments for National Public Radio, and as of 2007 she teaches in New York University's Cultural Reporting and Criticism program.*

In a disturbing marketing trend, video games are becoming more and more misogynistic. Games such as Grand Theft Auto: Vice City, *in which players regularly beat up and kill prostitutes, or* BMX XXX, *in which players can unlock footage of real-life strippers, push the envelope of decency in the gaming world. These games are troublesome when one considers current studies that show that people who view pornography hold misogynistic views against women in general. A connection has also been drawn between gender stereotyping and aggressive behavior. This knowledge, coupled with evidence that playing violent video games increases one's level of aggression, should raise concerns about the popularity of these sexist, often violent games.*

R ecently, a new addition to our household has taken up an enormous amount of my husband's time, drawn his friends to our apartment in elated droves, and reduced these grown men to sub-verbal states. No, unlike most young-

Lauren Sandler, "Game Boy," *New Republic*, vol. 228, no. 7, February 24, 2003, p. 38. Copyright © 2003 by The New Republic, Inc. Reproduced by permission of *The New Republic*.

marrieds in our neighborhood, we haven't added a baby to our family; we've added a gaming platform, on which my husband, Justin, and his friends have been playing a new breed of video games significantly racier than the joystick fantasies of our teens. The draw started with "Grand Theft Auto Vice City," which came out this fall and has my otherwise evolved friends and family running down hookers with stolen cars. But when I heard about "BMX XXX," sick curiosity and my internal homing device for hot spots in gender politics sent me straight to the video-game store.

Pushing the Limits on Standards of Decency

"BMX XXX" is a new game that simulates cycling. Sound boring? How about curvy women cycling in pasties and a thong? Justin and a friend devoted a recent afternoon to the virtual endeavor while I sipped vanilla tea and played occasional backseat driver (all for the sake of research, of course). In the game, you select every aspect of your player. If you choose to play as a female character, you get to customize her look—Jessica Rabbit red or Britney Spears pigtails, for instance. Our rider ended up as a brunette (that's Justin's personal preference) in pasties and a white lace thong (that's not, thank you). Setting the weight and proportion factors of our vixen, preprogrammed to be named "Hellkitty," we were able to get her down to 75 pounds—the game's estimate—without sacrificing her robust, D-cup curves. Then Hellkitty hopped on her bike, her rear bare but for a thread of white between the cheeks. Let the games begin! The mission is to accomplish a set of tasks, which range from innocuous bike tricks to serious acts of mayhem, like ramming over a hot-dog cart, doing errands for ne'er-do-wells, and picking up prostitutes on the back of your bike and delivering them to the local pimp. The reward for success in these half-pipe tricks isn't a high score; what you get for your wheelies and still-stands is footage of real-life topless strippers from Manhattan's infamous gentleman's establishment Scores and—if you do well enough—the chance to watch your player ride topless. If two people play, they can compete against each other in a variation on strip poker: The losing biker's clothing disappears garment by garment.

"BMX XXX" has many partners in misogyny in the world of video-play.

When the Parisian carriage-builder Pierre Lallement invented the bicycle in 1862 this was likely not what he had in mind. This new sport does more than challenge the standards of decency in the boys-will-be-boys world of gaming. By allowing boys (or grown men) to control a topless woman as their player, it could give a boost to both radical anti-porn feminists and conservatives who campaign against youth exposure to media violence and sex. Even the most radical anti-porn activists and theorists grant that the consumption of pornography—those lonely blue-glow moments—is an inherently passive thing, and historically it has been their burden to demonstrate how something so passive can connect with the active consequences they suggest: what scholar and activist Catharine MacKinnon calls "women's lesser entitlements—not to be raped, dehumanized, molested, invaded, and sold." In her book *Only Words*, MacKinnon argues that pornography constructs "the social reality of what a woman is and can be in terms of what can be done to her, and what a man is in terms of doing it." U.S. law and the larger society have taken a more libertarian view: Speech and conduct are different; porn has traditionally been the former and, importantly, not the latter. But, in this game, the player is both consumer and pornographer. The old divisions between speech and conduct are collapsed.

Misogynistic Beliefs Can Lead to Aggression

It's hard to find pornography studies not funded by a women's advocacy organization and therefore not geared toward demonstrating a link between viewing porn and sexually violent thoughts or behavior. But some exist, and they do bear out the feminist fear. Mike Allen, an associate professor of communication at the University of Wisconsin-Milwaukee found in a meta-analysis published in 1995 that pornography consumers tended to develop philosophies that absolved rapists of personal responsibility for their actions. Why does this matter? Because when you combine the effects of watching pornography with studies of video games and violence, you get a sense of the very real effect of the new cycling game. In the April 2000 *Journal of Personality and Social Psychology*, two studies under the umbrella title "Video Games and Aggressive Thoughts, Feelings, and Behavior in the Laboratory and in Life" found that violent video-game play outside the lab led to increased long-term aggressive behavior and delinquency, just as lab-based video-game experiments led to increased short-term aggressive behavior and thought. Interactivity—the inherent difference between video games and other forms of visual communication—is key to this development. According to "Fair Play," a 2001 study by the California-based liberal nonprofit group Children Now, "Video games' unique interactive capabilities may make them even more likely to influence children's attitudes, beliefs and behaviors than more traditional forms of media." And, not surprisingly, the effects measured in their study and others extend to "belief in gender stereotypes and increased aggressive behavior."

"BMX XXX" has many partners in misogyny in the world of video-play. "Grand Theft Auto" has boys genuflecting, parents hand-wringing, and Justin apologizing profusely when he boots up after dinner to deliver virtual hookers to their mobboss headquarters, occasionally bumping off a few streetwalkers along the way. The new "Dead or Alive Xtreme Beach Volleyball" closely emulates "BMX XXX" with its barely bikini-clad ballspikers, even outdoing "BMX"'s customizing option with a control that allows you to set the "jiggle factor" of your player's breasts. (The game is rumored to be offering a topless edition next season [as of 2003].) Next year will see the release of what may be the archetype of all subjugation games when Hugh Hefner unveils his game based on life at the Playboy Mansion. But, to date, "BMX XXX" is the industry leader.

In the conclusion to *Only Words*, MacKinnon imagines a day when "artifacts of these abuses will reside in a glass case next to the dinosaur skeletons in the Smithsonian" With "BMX XXX," sadly, that day seems quite a bit further off. And, when it comes, the glass case will have to fit not just video cameras and tapes but the discarded gaming platforms that delivered gender-training with a virtual dirt bike and a pornographic God complex.

10

Video Games Are Accepting More Gay-Themed Content

Jose Antonio Vargas

Jose Antonio Vargas is a staff writer for the Washington Post, *where he writes about the Internet and politics.*

Video games with gay characters and gay-themed content are becoming more common in the gaming market. Popular titles such as Bully allow players to choose whether their main character is gay. Although the game has already received criticism from "pro-family" groups and the Christian right, many game designers and game enthusiasts see the debut of gay characters in video games as a positive trend. For the most part, however, video games remain heterocentric, treating homosexuality more as a joke than an accepted way of life.

It's late on a school night at Bullworth Academy, a boarding school in New England. Young students Jimmy and Trent meet in a dark parking lot. "I've been waiting for this for a long time," Jimmy says, looking into Trent's eyes before telling him he's hot.

The two boys embrace, then kiss. There's a lot of moaning and a little bit of leg action. The scene is cheesy, the kind you might expect from a low-budget indie film about young gay love.

But this is not a film. It's a video game titled Bully—and it has caused a much bigger sensation than many gay-themed

Jose Antonio Vargas, "Coming Out of the Virtual Closet," *Advocate*, no. 978, January 16, 2007, pp. 62–64. Copyright © 2007 Jose Antonio Vargas. Reproduced by permission of Planet Out Inc.

movies. As films and television shows increasingly portray gay characters in a positive light, video games—with a sizable and tightly networked gay following—are finally starting to catch up.

Gay Characters Are Becoming More Common

Rockstar Games, the notoriously press-shy video game company that makes Bully, hasn't trumpeted the boy-on-boy tongue-twisting. It's simply there—the player's prerogative—and it's making a lot of gay gamers happy. "Hottest. Thing. Ever," read one verdict on GayGamer.net.

[P]arents might have a problem with their kids playing a game in which two boys can lock lips.

"It's surprising, in a good sort of way, making that option available and not making a big whoop about it," says Jeb Havens, 25, a lead designer for 1st Playable Productions and one of the few openly gay designers in the gaming industry. "Now, if only more games did that."

Indeed, Bully is a promising development in the video game industry: a big title from a big company starring a lead character who, depending on who plays the game, can be gay. It stars a 15-year-old toughie named Jimmy who, like any teen, must carefully navigate Bullworth Academy's social ladder—the jocks, the preppies, the nerds—to survive the year. He can give wedgies. He can befriend a nerd nicknamed Pee Stein. He can fight with a bully, hence the title. And if he so wishes, he can make out with certain boys just as he can make out with girls.

Far-right Christian leaders and "pro-family" groups were quick to condemn Bully. Conservative media watchdog Jack Thompson decried the game's "homosexual content" as "harmful to minors." Michael Patcher, a well-known video game analyst, added that parents might have a problem with their kids playing a game in which two boys can lock lips. And on the popular game site GameFAQs.com a player commented: "What is wrong with Rockstar? This is morally reprehensible."

While Jimmy may be the first gay game character to draw fire from antigay Christian forces, he joins a small but growing list of explicitly or ambiguously gay characters in video games. Bertram is an openly gay pirate in the port village of Nulb in the Temple of Elemental Evil, a role-playing game. Brad Evans is a tall, dark, and openly gay 30-something in Wild Arms 2, another role-playing game.

The jury's still out on whether Cybil Bennet of the horror game Silent Hill is a lesbian, but the motorcycle cop with leather pants and a don't-mess-with-me gaze has many gay game enthusiasts describing her as something right out of a Dykes on Bikes parade.

America may still be divided on the fight for marriage equality, but the battle was won two years ago in the most popular computer game of all time, The Sims. In the game's sequel, The Sims 2 same-sex Sims couples are allowed to wed without protest from straight Sims. Rod Humble, executive producer of the Sims 2, says the "general philosophy" of the game is "to prohibit as little as we have to." In the virtual world of the game Fable, men can court other men with flowers, chocolate, or even a house, and they can get married as well—but there's no physical contact between them.

Video Games Remain Mostly Heterocentric

While video gamers are not at all a monolithic crowd, gaming is widely perceived as the domain of young heterosexual men. And though it can be argued that games are the supreme form of escapism—on TV, you watch Will Truman; in a game, you are Will Truman—story lines in games have been largely heterocentric.

It may be an issue of who's making the games. According to a report by the International Game Developers Association, a San Francisco—based professional society, fewer than 6% of more than 6,000 recently surveyed game professionals identified as LGBT [lesbian, gay, bisexual, transgendered], and few of them are vocal about it.

There's still a long way to go, say both gay and straight game enthusiasts, in making games more gay-friendly.

Havens is one of those few. He has been speaking out about the importance of diversity in games, advocating the inclusion of gay characters and other progressive measures. Last March he organized the first LGBT round table at the Game Developers Conference in San Jose, Calif., which brought together a variety of straight and gay people in the video game world, including designers and programmers alongside student enthusiasts.

But despite Havens's efforts the heterocentric nature of video games may simply be a reflection of what is accepted by the majority of those who play and moderate the games. A controversy erupted earlier this year in the online swashbuckling fantasyland of World of Warcraft. Sara Andrews, writing on the game's message board, was trying to recruit members to her gay-friendly club. She was told she couldn't. Recruiting LGBT players was inappropriate, an online moderator for the game told her.

Weeks later, as gamers on sites such as Gaymer.org and Gamers.Experimentations.org protested, the makers of World of Warcraft apologized to Andrews and conducted "sensitivity training" workshops for its online moderators. In a phone interview Rob Pardo, the lead designer of the game, deemed the situation a "wake-up call."

There's still a long way to go, say both gay and straight game enthusiasts, in making games more gay-friendly. Says

Constance Steinkuehler, a University of Wisconsin-Madison professor whose research focuses on online role-playing games: "Fact is, game designers and game companies are largely not comfortable with the topic."

Flynn de Marco, a graphic designer who founded the site GayGamer.net, adds, "Gay characters in games are in the same place as gay characters in movies of the 1930s, '40s, '50s, even in the '70s. For the most part, gays are seen as a joke in games. 'Oh, look, I'm in a dress, I'm acting all fruity, ha ha ha!' Sadly, that's where we're at."

Which makes Jimmy, the lead character in Bully—which was released in October [2006] as one of the most anticipated games of the year—all the more intriguing. "That was really a risk for Rockstar," says Havens, "and I'm glad they did it."

11

Video Games Will Become More Artistically and Emotionally Satisfying

Jonathan Rauch

Jonathan Rauch is a senior writer and biweekly columnist for the National Journal, *a correspondent for the* Atlantic Monthly *and* Reason, *and a writer-in-residence at the Brookings Institution in Washington, DC.*

Interactive dramas show promise for being the new high-tech video games of the future. Similar to television soap operas or reality shows, these games feature stories revolving around virtual adult "actors" and adult relationships. Through incredible advances in artificial intelligence technology, players are able to communicate with the computer characters through ordinary English, as though having a true-to-life human conversation. Although this platform has yet to be perfected, the first game of this kind, Façade, has successfully drawn players into the storyline, tapping into their desire for an emotional connection with the game's characters, rather than the more traditional gamers need for action. While it will be left to future consumers to ultimately decide if interactive dramas are "fun" enough to sustain sales, those sampling the dramas in their early stages agree that, like the characters of great literature, the actors in interactive dramas have the potential to live on in players' minds.

Jonathan Rauch, "Sex, Lies, and Video Games," *Atlantic Monthly,* vol. 298, no. 4, November 2006, pp. 76–82. www.theatlantic.com/doc/prem/200611/rauch-videogames. Copyright © 2006 The Atlantic Monthly Magazine. Reproduced by permission.

What if a computer program combined the action and graphics of a video game with the emotional power of great art? The result could revolutionize interactive entertainment—and even change the meaning of "play."

Michael Mateas is the sort of person who once built an artificially intelligent(ish) robot houseplant that monitored your e-mail and changed shape to reflect the mood of what it read—if that sort of person can be said to be a sort. This was in 1998, when Mateas was a doctoral student with some avant-garde ideas. Office Plant #1, as the creation was called, grew and shrank and blossomed and hibernated and waved its piano-wire fronds as it "fed" off e-mail traffic. Naturally, it also whistled, sang, moaned, and complained. Not long after building Office Plant #1, however, Mateas set it aside. He became interested in bigger things, like creating a new art form.

Meanwhile, Andrew Stern, a programmer and designer at a now-defunct [as of 2006] video-game studio, was building artificially intelligent(ish) virtual pets. They were called Petz, and for a while they were a hit in the video-game industry. First came Dogz, in 1995, then Catz, and eventually Babyz, all adorable animated creatures that lived on your computer's hard drive. As Stern worked on making the virtual creatures emotionally appealing and realistic to play with, he began giving them artificial minds: goals, personalities, memories. It dawned on him that he wanted to work with adult characters in lifelike relationships. He became interested in bigger things, like creating a new art form.

Entering this world [of an interactive drama], you would feel as if you had been thrust into the midst of a soap opera or a reality-TV show.

Not long after Petz debuted, Stern began attending some of the same conferences on artificial intelligence that Mateas haunted. It was probably inevitable that Stern, presenting his intelligent(ish) virtual pets, would run into Mateas, presenting his intelligent(ish) robot plant. It didn't take long for them to recognize each other as kindred spirits.

Interactive Drama

In certain rarefied circles of AI [artificial intelligence] academia and video-game design, people sometimes theorize about a computer program that would combine the graphical realism of a modern video game with the emotional impact of great art. "Interactive drama," the concept is called. It might contain artificial people you could converse with, get to know, and love or hate. It might engineer dramatic situations, complete with revelations and reversals. Entering this world, you would feel as if you had been thrust into the midst of a soap opera or a reality-TV show.

"I had some idea how to do it," Stern says. Mateas, for his part, had dreamed since childhood of building artificial humans. It occurred to him that he could advance his dream by building artificial actors. What better way to teach a computer to act human, after all, than by teaching it to act?

Almost three-quarters of the best-selling games on the market are in the fighting, shooting, racing, action, and sports genres.

In 1998, emerging from a hot tub at a conference in Snowbird, Utah, Mateas and Stern decided to collaborate. "As Andrew and I talked," Mateas recalls, "we sort of egged each other on to jump as far out of the mainstream as possible." They resolved to create a game that would put a *not* in front of every convention of today's video-game industry. They looked upon their game as a research project and figured that building it would take two years. It took more than five. Now they are starting on a larger version, this time a commercial game.

A Need for Innovation

They think interactive drama has the potential to be to this century what cinema was to the last. When I spent a couple of days getting to know them recently, I asked why they're not trying something more modest, such as making the characters in today's video games more lifelike. "That's a sort of incremental innovation that I think neither of us is interested in," Mateas replied. "We're interested in revolutionary innovation."

If today's video-game industry were a person, it would be at what people used to call "that awkward age." Suddenly, like a teenager with long legs and short pants, it finds itself grossing $31 billion this year in revenues worldwide, according to the business consultancy Pricewaterhouse Coopers, and nearly $10 billion in the United States alone. If the industry keeps up its growth, Pricewaterhouse expects it to rival the global recorded-music business by about 2010. Yet the video-game industry, for all its swagger and success, remains something of a niche player. In the United States, it is smaller than the theme-park and amusement-park industry; according to Price Waterhouse, its rapid growth would still leave it, in 2010, about a third the size of the film, radio, or book industry, and about a seventh the size of the television industry.

A lot of people play games now, and not just kids: the average gamer, according to the Entertainment Software Association [ESA], is thirty-three years old. But while just about everyone regularly listens to music or reads books or watches movies, many adults never pick up a joystick. Only about a seventh of game titles sold in 2005 were the racy or violent stuff that draws an M (for "mature") rating; the stereotype that video games are nothing but antisocial savagery is just that—a stereotype. Puzzles, pets, strategy games, and social games abound. But it's true that the adrenaline-pumping, youth-oriented genres dominate. According to the ESA, almost three-quarters of the best-selling games on the market are in the fighting, shooting, racing, action, and sports genres. A sexist commentator might call it boy stuff.

The graphics of the best modern games are stunning, and their "physics"—their power to create a world that feels real as you move about in it—hardly less so. But the industry is rife with game designers who complain of "sequelitis" and creative underachievement. "Will we address an excruciatingly audience-limiting lack of diversity in our content?" wondered Warren Spector, one of the industry's leading developers, in a recent article in *The Escapist*, a video-game magazine. "I can see us limiting ourselves to the same subset of adolescent male players we've always reached. And if we do that, it's back to the margins for us."

If video games seem inhuman, that is because they lack humans.

"There's no drama genre, there's no comedy genre," Andrew Stern told me recently. "What exists right now are action movies, basically." He might have added: silent action movies. The video-game industry's annual trade show in Los Angeles, called the Electronic Entertainment Expo, or E3 for short, is one of the loudest places I have ever been. Also one of the most silent.

Most Video Games Lack Human Conversation

This year's [2006] show occupied all of L.A.'s cavernous convention center. Its thousands of microprocessors and liquid crystal displays and sound systems burned enough electricity to power a good-sized suburb. Take the crowds of Times Square, add the high-tech dazzle of Tokyo and the floor-shaking decibels of surround-sound cinema, throw in Vegas-style showgirls (known in the trade as "booth babes"), and you have some idea of E3.

Drifting through the show last May, I saw many shallow games and many derivative games: superheroes dueling with giant robots, skateboarders flashing Nike logos, boxers throwing punches amid showers of sweat and spittle, warriors trudging through jungles and snowscapes. Joining one particularly long line, I found myself in a small, darkened room where a designer was debating Midway's John Woo Presents: Stranglehold. Fighters were demolishing everything in sight. "Look at the state of the teahouse, just massive destruction," said the designer lovingly. "And it never looks the same twice." As he emphasized how realistically each bullet splintered the walls, a male connoisseur in the audience called out, "Aim for the head!" (The audience in this demo, and at the show generally, was at least 80 percent male.) Even the schlock, however, exhibited striking craft and ingenuity, and I came across some astonishingly imaginative games, including an alien-invasion shooter (Capcom's Lost Planet: Extreme Condition) whose visuals were so compelling that I was helpless to tear myself away.

It was only after I left the hall that I realized there was something odd about all the noise. The thunderous sound effects were masking the absence of conversation. In real life, much of what's interesting involves talking to people. The characters in games could deliver scripted lines like "I'm ready to kick some ass!" or drop prerecorded comments on the action, but conversing with me or each other was completely beyond them. It occurred to me that if video games seem inhuman, that is because they lack humans. Their esoteric syntax is an artifact of a stunted environment in which blasting someone's head off is easy but talking to him is impossible.

Meaning Requires Words

A month later, I asked Andrew Stern what he thinks of E3. "I shake my head a little," he replied. "All this effort and money being poured into all this derivative and uninspired work. I'm bored and slightly disgusted." Few in the mainstream industry would express disgust with their product, but many designers, being intelligent and creative people, feel they have made much less of their powerful medium than it could be. They are vexed by a sense of underachievement. As Will Wright, the most famous and successful American game designer, told a crowded session at E3, "Interactive design is a really large box, and we've really only explored one little tiny corner of that box." David Cage, another prominent designer, told another audience, "What strikes me in this industry is, there's just a real lack of meaning in general."

Instead of offering the players menus of quests or options, their game would seem to flow as naturally as life.

Meaning is the catalyst that turns action to drama. Meaning requires words, not just sounds. It requires characters, not just figures. It requires dramatic shape: a sense that the action is leading to some transformation or resolution. It is what Stern and Mateas resolved they would bring to video games. . . .

By the time their paths crossed, their thinking had already converged. They soon began plotting their anti-game. Instead of making a game about action figures in elaborate but childish game-worlds, they would make a story about adult characters and adult relationships. Instead of firing bullets at the characters, the player would fire words. The player would talk to the characters—in ordinary English, input with a keyboard rather than a joystick. And the characters would talk back, to each other and to the player. This meant—and they gulped to think of it—that their game would need to speak and understand natural language. That, in itself, is one of the great challenges in AI. But they didn't intend to stop there.

Interactive Dramas
Need Interactive Language

Conventional games create vast, immersive physical environments. The new game would all take place in a single indoor space, like a black-box theater stage. Instead of taking fifty hours to play, their game would take twenty minutes. Instead of advancing through levels without telling a story, the game would provide a compact, complete dramatic experience, like a one-act play. "We envisioned something where you could come home from work and play it from beginning to end, just like you come home from work and watch a half-hour television show," said Mateas. "You could come home and have a half-hour interactive-drama experience. It's complete in itself, it takes you on an arc. It entertains. But then the next day, you could come home from work and play it again and make something different happen." Instead of offering the player menus of quests or options, their game would seem to flow as naturally as life.

When Mateas, still a graduate student, told his adviser what they intended, the adviser replied that such a game would take a team of ten people ten years to build. The technology didn't exist. Commercial game design often employs teams of dozens, and here were two guys, one a grad student and the other self-employed (Stern eventually quit his job to work on the game full-time), expecting to build a whole new kind of game with their own four hands and no budget to speak of.

Before they could build the game, they had to build a programming language in which to write it. They spent more than two years constructing what they called ABL (for "A Behavior Language"), which encodes and controls virtual actors, "The actors' minds are written in ABL," Mateas explains. ABL itself has a sort of mind: enough artificial intelligence to decide how a particular character might, for example, simultaneously mix a drink, walk across the room, and yell at her husband, as a human actor could do.

Movies and Literature Influence Dramatic Games

That done, they built, again from scratch, another piece of AI, which they call a drama manager. It is a sort of artificial dramaturge and director, which looks at what the player and characters are doing and makes plot and dialogue choices intended to ratchet up and then release dramatic tension. Then they built a natural-language engine, which "listens" to what the player types in, looking for emotional and dramatic cues that the in-game characters can react to.

The game, by now, packed massive amounts of experimental technology under its hood, but what would it be about? They needed to create an intense drama in a confined space and with only a few characters. Influenced by Edward Albee's play *Who's Afraid of Virginia Woolf?* and also by several movies (Steven Soderbergh's *Sex, Lies, and Videotape*, Woody Allen's *Husbands and Wives*, and Ingmar Bergman's *Scenes from a Marriage*), they decided to drop the player into a marital crisis. They hired actors to record five hours of dialogue, raw material from which the drama manager would build twenty minutes of game play.

In the end, they accomplished, they reckon, about 30 percent of what they had hoped to do. "We shot for the stars in hopes of getting to the moon," says Stern, "and we made it into orbit." In July 2005, standing together over Stern's computer in Portland, they pressed the button that "shipped," over the Internet, a new game called Façade.

Even the Most High-Tech Games Are Flawed

When I set out to report this article, I thought I would bone up on video games and present myself as a suave expert. After all, I used to play a lot of Tetris. My aspirations to coolness lasted about three minutes, which was how long it took to load Electronic Arts' NBA Live 06. Jake Snyder, a twenty-something employee of the Entertainment Software Association, handed me the controls of a Microsoft Xbox 360 game console while two startlingly realistic basketball teams took shape before my eyes. As I stabbed at the unfamiliar buttons, I could barely control the ball. Flailing, I became aware that the game's: color commentators were talking about . . . me. No, correction: they were mocking me. "Nice easy attempt, but they just can't make a shot," they said. "Totally disorganized," they sneered. I realized, face burning, that I had just lost the respect of a software product.

State-of-the-art games render action and environment with eerie realism and genuine aesthetic distinction. But their characters are dolls, not people.

Determined to endure any further humiliations in private, I bought a copy of a critically acclaimed single-player game called The Elder Scrolls IV: Oblivion, a big hit from Bethesda Softworks and a new threshold of accomplishment in its genre. It came with a fifty-page manual full of instructions like this: "DISPEL: Removes Magicka-based spell effects from the target. Does not affect abilities, diseases, curses, or constant magic item effects. The magnitude of the Dispel must exceed the spell's resistance to dispel (based on its casting cost) in order to dispel it." I despaired. This sounded about as fun as learning Microsoft Windows.

Entering the game, I was at first mystified and frustrated, but before long I was slaying goblins and pilfering valuables and casting spells and exploring caves. As the hours went by, I felt myself drawn in, then immersed, then reluctant to leave. I felt I was in the presence of a powerful medium, nothing like Tetris.

Oblivion's world is vast. A company spokesman told me I could explore for 500 hours before seeing everything. The game enfolded me in lush, cinematic landscapes. It populated the cities, changed the weather, cycled through day and night.

Looking down I saw grass rendered in granular detail; looking up I saw skies swept with feathery clouds; all around me I found innumerable creatures and towns and terrains. The illusion was magical.

But then it would all collapse. Approaching one of the characters, I would click for dialogue. The character would give a little canned speech introducing itself. In response to another click, it would mouth several bits of prerecorded dialogue. State-of-the-art games render action and environment with eerie realism and genuine aesthetic distinction. But their characters are dolls, not people.

Interactive Dramas Require Players' Participation

It took me no more than a couple of minutes to see that Façade would be different. Grace and Trip, a married couple and old friends of mine, invite me over. He's blond, she's brunette, they seem to be in their thirties. As I arrive, I hear them arguing behind the door. After I knock, I'm cordially admitted by Trip into a small, sparsely furnished apartment with a view of towering apartment blocks glowing against a night sky.

Typing "Hi, Grace, you look great," I begin chatting with the couple. They try to draw me into their simmering argument, nudging me to take sides. I can say anything I like; there are no rules. I can be sullen and unresponsive (that got me kicked out of their apartment), or I can talk nonsense, but in most of my visits I try to behave like an improv actor, picking up on their lines and shooting back cues of my own—agreeing with one, criticizing the other, flirting with either or both. No two plays are identical. In a typical game, however, Grace and Trip will argue with each other, one may flatter me while the other questions my friendship, and the tension between them will build until feelings are raw and the story reaches a revelation or a breaking point. Here I'm playing as Ed:

TRIP: Okay, you know what, Ed, I need to ask you something.

GRACE: Trip—

ED: What?

TRIP: Grace, let me ask our guest a question. Ed, yes or no—

ED: Let him ask, Grace.

TRIP: Each person in a marriage is supposed to try really hard to be in sync with the other, right?

GRACE: What?

TRIP: I mean, when you're married, to make it good, you need to always be positive, and agreeable, and together, right?

ED: [Hesitates.]

TRIP: Yes or no.

ED: No, not always.

GRACE: What?! Oh, all right. Yes. Just admit it, Trip, admit it, we have a shitty marriage! We've never been really happy, from day one! Never, goddammit!

"There is a huge untapped market for experiences that are not about action adventures, quests, killing monsters, and solving puzzles."

Here the drama manager is raising the tension to prepare for a revelation; notice how it demands my participation. The game can end in reconciliation or a split or, sometimes, neither. This time, Grace reveals that she let Trip stop her from becoming an artist, and Trip realizes his mistake, and they reconcile. "Ed, thanks for coming over," Trip tells me, his voice now subdued. "You—I think you helped us." I exit; the game is over. Next time, something quite different will happen.

Façade Affects Players' Emotions

Façade won the grand jury prize at this year's Slamdance independent-game festival and has drawn wide notice from industry journalists and bloggers. . . . So far, more than

350,000 people have [downloaded it]. Play and decide for yourself—but for me, playing Façade was both uncanny and frustrating.

Uncanny because Grace and Trip, despite being simply drawn, are at moments shockingly natural. "It was so subtle, was what impressed me," Will Wright, the prominent game designer, said when I asked him about Façade. "Most games beat you over the head with explosions and life-and-death situations and saving the world. And this is so subtle!" Trip, he marveled, can be slightly annoyed. "The fact that a character could be slightly annoyed in a game!"

Frustrating because, for all their innovative AI-driven mechanics, Grace and Trip remain too dumb to sustain the illusion of humanness. When I played as a woman (I could choose my sex) and announced I was pregnant with Trip's child, Grace and Trip thought I was flirting with them. They really only guess at a player's meaning, and they don't guess very well. "It kind of works," says Doug Church, a respected designer with Electronic Arts, the 800-pound gorilla of U.S. video-game publishers. "It has moments of awesomeness. It has moments of Wow, if I could play that, I'd be so excited! But then you try the next step and bam! You hit a wall and the wrong thing happens."

Yet when it does work, when the game flows and the player has figured out how to collaborate with Grace and Trip, there are those moments. After a successful performance (to call it a game seems wrong), I jotted this note: "I feel a strange desire to please these characters and, despite my better judgment, touched when Grace reveals she's scared of painting and they reconcile." Façade feels like the small-scale, no-budget, first-try research project that it is. But it was still capable of working on my emotions.

Big Plans for Interactive Dramas

In January [2006], at Slamdance, Mateas and Stern met some investors who were excited about interactive drama. Many phone conversations later, they had a deal to raise $2 million for a commercial game. This was a crucial step for them. Stern, in particular, sees himself heading a commercial interactive-drama studio. Both he and Mateas believe that today's video games occupy only a fraction of the potential market for interactive-video entertainment.

"Most people—your sort of regular Joe or Jane on the street who loves television and movies—don't really get a whole lot out of games," Stern said, when I asked who would buy interactive dramas.

"I think there's a real market for more character-rich, story-centered interactive experiences," Mateas added. "I think potentially it's a market that dwarfs the entire current video-game market. There is a huge untapped market for experiences that are not about action adventures, quests, killing monsters, and solving puzzles."

In The Party, violence will be rare and dramatically meaningful, ricocheting through the game, as in life, with unforeseen consequences.

Developing The Party

They have given their next game the working title "The Party." It is still in the conceptual stage, but they expect that, where Façade had two computer-generated characters, The Party will have ten, a far more complicated proposition, but dramatically richer. It will require not just two programmers but, once it enters production, ten or more. The graphics will be more detailed and polished. The action will take place in a larger space. The game will last about forty minutes, rather than twenty. It will support more physical action, allowing the player to do things like rendezvous with characters in a private room, lock doors, carry things around, and fire a weapon.

It will, they expect, understand the player better than Façade does, and support many more player moves.

And its aesthetic will be different. If Façade is a psychological drama, The Party will be a darkly comic social melodrama, along the lines of Desperate Housewives. In the prototype scripts, you find yourself cohosting a dinner party with your wife (or husband, if you play as a woman), who begs you to keep the conversation and liquor flowing smoothly. As guests arrive, the party fills with characters who have various designs on you and on each other. Your ex-girlfriend may try to break up your marriage; her angry husband may deck you; your neighbor may be snooping and your boss fishing for excuses to fire you. You can try to keep everyone happy, or you can hurl insults, or seduce your best friend's wife, or announce that you're gay, or refuse to admit guests (in which case your wife may let them in while shooting you angry looks), or lock your boss in the basement. You can try to mind your own business and be left alone. At every stage, however, the other characters—and behind them the drama manager—are conniving to draw you in. Madcap complications ensue.

There will be sex in the game, and there will be violence. There will be a gun, but only one bullet, so no shoot-outs. Here again, the designers invert the conventions of VideoGame Land, where shooting people is easy but talking to them is hard: in The Party, violence will be rare and dramatically meaningful, ricocheting through the game, as in life, with unforeseen consequences. Sex, likewise, will be dramatic rather than pornographic. It may disrupt a marriage or get someone killed. The sex will not be X-rated, but it will be realistic. "You may not literally see it, but the characters will be moaning," Stern said.

Mateas and Stern expect work on The Party to take two and a half years, at least. They hope to make the game a paying franchise and use the proceeds to push on toward their real goal: a game that understands natural language and generates its own drama.

The Party, like Façade, will assemble bits of prerecorded dialogue and preauthored plot points, the drama manager, as if stringing beads, will sequence the bits as it monitors the action, in the end, the game can be no bigger than its supply of prefabricated dramatic possibilities. The door to a world of truly open-ended drama will unlock only when a computer learns to write its own dialogue and plot twists, using rules that teach it to emulate a human playwright or screenwriter.

I raised an eyebrow. Can it be done? A simple prototype, Mateas said, is "totally doable within twenty years."

"We have every intention of doing those projects," Stern added.

A Respectful Curiosity

The mainstream video-game industry is interested in hits, not research. On the business side of the industry, none of the executives I talked to had heard of Mateas and Stern, and the executives tended to regard the interactive-drama project, when I described it, with polite skepticism, or—off the record—not-so-polite skepticism. "People love to blow shit up," one told me. He acknowledged exceptions, but said, "Blowing shit up is fundamental, because verbs are what make video games work. These guys are not going to succeed." At E3, I mentioned the Mateas-Stern project to Mitch Lasky, who himself has defied industry skepticism by making a fortune on cell-phone games. (He is now with Electronic Arts.) By way of response, he took a long drag on an imaginary marijuana joint. Good luck, was his attitude—but he wouldn't invest.

In the smaller world of game designers, by contrast, Mateas and Stern are a known commodity and are regarded with something like respectful curiosity. Designers have seen too many artificial-intelligence failures to expect any kind of revolution, but at this point they would be happy if characters just got smarter. "A lot of people have worked on it," Doug Church, of Electronic Arts, told me. "Every year we're like, 'We're going to design incredibly intelligent, fluid humans who act realistically.' We try to take this huge step—and we fall all the way back down. At least," he said of Mateas and Stern, "they ended up somewhere new. It doesn't all work, but it is at least a step."

"It's a really hard problem, but it's one that we're incrementally going to solve," Will Wright mused, when I asked him about creating believable characters. "It's a very tall mountain we're climbing." Mateas and Stern, he added, don't have the answer, but they have found a path uphill.

To my astonishment within five minutes I was comfortably building a scaly, beaked alien, as lavishly detailed and three-dimensional as anything one might see in a Pixar movie.

The Maker of Sims Offers Something New

At the moment, all industry eyes are on a project of Wright's, one that enjoys EA's multimillion-dollar backing. (EA owns Wright's studio, Maxis.) Wright is nearing completion of a game called Spore, expected some time next year. His last game, The Sims, was the biggest computer-game hit of all time and a major innovation in its own right. Spore, as a feat of creative imagination and technical prowess, outdoes The Sims handily. It has enjoyed extravagant media hype for a game that has yet to ship a single unit. All I can say, having test-driven it, is that the hype understates the case.

Like Façade and The Party, Spore inverts traditional industry rules—but a different set of industry rules. Instead of outfitting the computer with a vast, prefabricated world for the player to explore, it leaves the designing of worlds to the players. But there is nothing, really, to "play": no need to win or compete. Instead, the player begins with a microbe, then helps it evolve into a creature of the player's own design. The creature spawns and becomes intelligent, eventually forming tribes and populating the planet; the player can then zoom out to explore a universe of planets and creatures, all created by other users and downloaded into his game from a mighty central server at Electronic Arts. In Spore, as Carl Sagan might have said, there are millions and millions of planets, all the fanciful, scary, inspired, or insipid handiwork of thousands or millions of players.

At E3, after watching Will Wright demonstrate the game to a couple dozen people in a small room with black walls, I was shown into an even smaller black room, where I sat down in front of an ordinary PC and went to work designing my own creature. To my astonishment within five minutes I was comfortably building a scaly, beaked alien, as lavishly detailed and three-dimensional as anything one might see in a Pixar movie. Once I had given it enough body parts to move, it began . . . moving! It hopped. It walked. It made me giggle. Spore's most notable technical achievement is to teach the computer to animate whatever sort of creature anybody might design. Five legs? A buzz saw-tipped tail and eyes astride the neck? No problem; the software, as if channeling Chuck Jones, looks at what you build and brings it to life, complete with characteristic movement, expressions, and even babies of the species. With not much more effort, I next terra-formed a planet, giving it candy-colored mountains and icy lakes. It was as if I had a whole animation studio in my right hand.

Spore looks nothing like Façade and The Party. It is mainstream and big budget instead of independent and cheap, freeform in structure and timescale (you could play forever) instead of tightly woven and compact, visual instead of verbal (there are no people or words in Spore). It is, however, in some respects another bite from the same apple: born partly of frustration with the crippling limitations of existing video games, all three products seek to create a new audience for video-game play by redefining the meaning of video-game "play": play not as competition within rules (as in "play Tetris"), but play as creative fun (Spore is, at heart, a fantastically powerful toy) or play as dramatic performance (Façade and The Party are, at heart, interactive theater). Spore, if it succeeds, will evoke in the player a feeling of magical delight. Interactive drama, if it succeeds, will evoke emotional catharsis.

Consumers Want Games that Are Fun

But how many consumers of entertainment actually want catharsis, especially after a long day at work? What most consumers of entertainment want is fun. The story goes that Will Wright was once approached by a designer who pitched a game that featured an elaborate new enemy system. As Heather Chaplin and Aaron Ruby relate the incident in their history of video games, *Smartbomb*, Wright heard out the pitch and then deflated the guy with one devastating sentence. "Hmm" he said, "that doesn't sound very fun."

Façade is ingenious, but it is not fun. It isn't really meant to be. The Party may turn out to be fun, even funny. But authoring fun is hard, and it is not obvious that interactive drama is a natural route to funness.

A game, even a great game, is finished once played, but a great character, once met, lives forever.

When the question of fun comes up, Mateas and Stern turn a little defensive. They are quick to say that games like Tony Hawk's Pro Skater, X-Men Legends, and Destroy All Humans! will always be with us, which is fine by them. They just want to do more. Mateas said, "When you go and see an intense movie or a seriously intense play, you don't walk out and go. 'God, that was fun!' It was a valuable experience and something you wanted to do and got something out of, but what you got out of it wasn't 'fun.' It was thoughtful, reflective, made you think about your own life, made you think about the human condition, moved you. And I think interactive media can do exactly the same thing, and potentially more powerfully than noninteractive media."

I asked what sort of aesthetic experience they had in mind. "Making players feel a true connection to characters on the screen." Stern replied. "You'd feel like you're immersed in an actual relationship with these characters."

"Yeah," added Mateas. "Having the player actually care about the characters."

They may be wrong about the commercial market for whatever they wind up creating, but they must be right about the human appetite for characters. A game, even a great game, is finished once played, but a great character, once met, lives forever. Think of Sherlock Holmes and Mr. Spock, Don Quixote and Captain Ahab, Holden Caulfield and Humbert Humbert, Scrooge and Gandalf, Charlie Brown and Severus Snape.

In your mind, then, take the animation intelligence of Spore and the dramatic intelligence of Façade, increase their sophistication by orders of magnitude, and extend both vectors until they intersect. Imagine a game that could conjure a Holmes or a Spock, or that could create, or empower the player to create, all manner of original characters, each character not only animated but personified: acted. Imagine a game that not only conjured the cobblestones of Victorian London or the red sky of Vulcan but that charged each city, each planet, with a quantum of dramatic potential. Imagine, at last, entering those dramas and encountering those characters. Games, if such they were, might be as short as a sitcom episode or as long as a soap-opera season; characters might be ones you created, bought, traded, or downloaded on a friend's recommendation; genres might span everything from comedy and fantasy to mystery and tragedy. You might not even need to choose: the software might watch how you play, learn your taste, and create dramas and characters and worlds to order. "Twenty years from now," Will Wright likes to say, "games will be as personal to you as your dreams, and as emotionally deep and meaningful to you as your dreams."

Organizations to Contact

The editors have compiled the following list of organizations concerned with the issues debated in this book. The descriptions are derived from materials provided by the organizations. All have publications or information available for interested readers. The list was compiled on the date of publication of the present volume; the information provided here may change. Be aware that many organizations take several weeks or longer to respond to inquiries, so allow as much time as possible.

American Psychological Association
Office of Public Affairs, 750 First St. NE
Washington, DC   20002-4242
(800) 374-2721
e-mail: public.affairs@apa.org
Web site: www.apa.org

The mission of the American Psychological Association (APA) is to "advance psychology as a science, as a profession, and as a means of promoting human welfare." As part of its commitment to social welfare, APA investigates the potential link between violent video games and increased aggression in children. Its Web site includes press releases about violence in video games as well as archived essays such as "Violent Video Games: Myths, Facts, and Unanswered Questions."

Center for Successful Parenting
e-mail: csp@onrampamerica.net
Web site: www.sosparents.org

The Center for Successful Parenting believes that violent video games have a negative impact on child development. The organization stresses grassroots activism to eliminate the marketing of violent media to children. The Center's Web site offers information on game ratings and a few studies showing the detrimental effect violent video games have on brain development.

Children Now

1212 Broadway, 5th Floor, Oakland, CA   94612

(510) 763-2444 • fax: (510) 763-1974

e-mail: info@childrennow.org

Web site: www.childrennow.org

Children Now is an independent, nonpartisan organization that seeks to ensure the interests of children are protected in public policy issues. Part of its goal is to improve the quality of entertainment media aimed at children. Its Web site archives some articles relating to video games and the ratings system designed to match games to children's maturity levels.

Common Sense Media

1550 Bryant St., Suite 555, San Francisco, CA   94103

(415) 863-0600

Web site: www.commonsensemedia.org

Common Sense Media is devoted to improving the media experiences of children and families. It advocates media literacy rather than censorship to help children and parents navigate the barrage of media influences that impact people daily. The organization offers reviews of video games and other media products on its Web site.

Computer Addiction Services

McLean Hospital, 115 Mill St., Belmont, MA   02478

(617) 855-2908

e-mail: orzack@computeraddiction.com

Web site: www.computeraddiction.com

Funded by clinical psychologist Maressa Hecht Orzack, Computer Addiction Services maintains that excessive computer use is similar to substance abuse. Computer Addiction Services claims that people are becoming more computer dependent for both information and entertainment and that this addictive behavior is problematic for individuals and society.

Entertainment Consumers Association

64 Danbury Rd., Suite 700, Wilton, CT   06897-4406
(203) 761-6180 • fax: (203) 761-6184
e-mail: feedback@theeca.com
Web site: www.theeca.com

The Entertainment Consumers Association (ECA) is a non-profit organization designed to serve the needs of video game players through advocacy, consumer rights initiatives, and political lobbying. The ECA Web site includes position papers on violence in video games, video games regulations, and safe play in online games. ECA also distributes an online newsletter regarding the industry and consumer events.

Entertainment Software Association

575 Seventh St. NW, Suite 300, Washington, DC   20004
e-mail: esa@theesa.com
Web site: www.theesa.com

The Entertainment Software Association (ESA) is an American association exclusively dedicated to serving the business and public affairs needs of video game companies. The ESA Web site offers a comprehensive "Essential Facts about Games and Court Rulings" article and various position papers on violence in video games.

Entertainment Software Rating Board

317 Madison Ave., 22nd Floor, New York, NY   10017
Web site: www.esrb.org

Established in 1994, the Entertainment Software Rating Board (ESRB) is a nonprofit regulatory board created by the Entertainment Software Association. The board rates video games based on content and the targeted age group. Game-specific ratings are available on the Web site. The ESRB site also contains information pages on recent industry news, parent and consumer protection, and education and outreach programs.

International Game Developers Association

19 Mantua Rd., Mt. Royal, NJ   08061
(856) 423-2990 • fax: (856) 423-3420
e-mail: contact@igda.org
Web site: www.igda.org

The International Game Developers Association (IGDA) is an industry association that promotes career development and fosters community interests within the field of video game design. Part of the IGDA mission is to fight censorship of video games. The IGDA Web site includes some position papers on concerns over video game rating and censorship. It also publishes the *IGDA Newsletter.*

National Institute on Media and the Family

606 Twenty-fourth Ave. S, Suite 606
Minneapolis, MN   55454
(888) 672-5437 • fax: (612) 672-4113
Web site: www.mediafamily.org

The National Institute on Media and the Family is a nonprofit, nonpartisan organization that provides research, education, and information concerning the impact of media on children and families. The goal of the organization is to empower parents and other consumers to make informed choices about media products that will likely impact children. The institute's Web Site provides some information on video game violence and video game addiction.

Bibliography

Books

Craig A. Anderson, Douglas A. Gentile, and Katherine E. Buckley

Violent Video Game Effects on Children and Adolescents: Theory, Research, and Public Policy. New York: Oxford University Press, 2007.

John C. Beck and Mitchell Wade

Got Game: How the Gamer Generation Is Reshaping Business Forever. Boston: Harvard Business School Press, 2004.

Ian Bogost

Unit Operations: An Approach to Videogame Criticism. Cambridge, MA: MIT Press, 2006.

Olivia Bruner and Kurt Bruner

Playstation Nation: Protect Your Child from Video Game Addiction. New York: Center Street, 2006.

Edward Castronova

Synthetic Worlds: The Business and Culture of Online Games. Chicago: University of Chicago Press, 2005.

Heather Chaplin and Aaron Ruby

Smartbomb: The Quest for Art, Entertainment, and Big Bucks in the Videogame Revolution. Chapel Hill, NC: Algonquin, 2006.

Rusel DeMaria

Reset: Changing the Way We Look at Video Games. San Francisco: Berrett-Koehler Publishers, 2007.

James Paul Gee
What Video Games Have to Teach Us about Learning and Literacy. New York: Palgrave McMillan, 2004.

Dave Grossman and Gloria DeGaetano
Stop Teaching Our Kids to Kill: A Call to Action Against TV, Movie and Video Game Violence. New York: Crown, 1999.

Steven Johnson
Everything Bad Is Good for You: How Today's Popular Culture Is Actually Making Us Smarter. New York: Riverhead Trade, 2006.

Jesper Juul
Half-Real: Video Games between Real Rules and Fictional Worlds. Cambridge, MA: MIT Press, 2005.

Steven L. Kent
The Ultimate History of Video Games: From Pong to Pokemon and Beyond— The Story Behind the Craze Ttat Touched Our Lives and Changed the World. Roseville, CA: Prima, 2001.

Bill Maier
Help! My Child Is Hooked on Video Games. Colorado Springs, CO: Focus on the Family, 2006.

David Williamson Shaffer
How Computer Games Help Children Learn. New York: Palgrave Macmillan, 2007.

T.L. Taylor
Play Between Worlds: Exploring Online Game Culture. Cambridge, MA: MIT Press, 2006.

Peter Vorderer
and Jennings
Bryant, eds.
Playing Video Games: Motives, Responses, and Consequences. Mahwah, NJ: Lawrence Erlbaum Associates, 2006.

Mark J.P. Wolf
and Bernard
Perron
The Video Game Theory Reader. New York: Routledge, 2003.

Periodicals

Jane Avrich,
Steven Johnson,
Raph Koster, et al.
"Grand Theft Education: Literacy in the Age of Video Games," *Harper's*, September 2006.

Pippin Barr,
James Noble, and
Robert Biddle
"Video Game Values: Human—Computer Interaction and Games," *Interacting with Computers*, March 2007.

Rhea R. Borja
"Video Games Trickle from Rec Rooms to Classrooms," *Education Week*, December 6, 2006.

Erika Brown
"Game On!" *Forbes*, July 24, 2006.

Nicholas L.
Carnagey, Craig
A. Anderson, and
Brad J. Bushman
"The Effect of Video Game Violence on Physiological Desensitization to Real-Life Violence," *Journal of Experimental Social Psychology*, May 2007.

Heather Chaplin
"Video Games Tests the Limits. The Limits Win," *New York Times*, January 28, 2007.

Bruce Cole and
Steven Johnson
"When Oliver Twist Meets Grand Theft Auto," *Humanities*, November–December 2006.

Lisa Selin Davis   "Click Here to Create a Better
                       World," *On Earth: Environmental
                       Politics People*, Spring 2007.

Dave Gilson   "Even Better than the Real Thing,"
                       Mother Jones, May–June 2007.

Ed Halter   "Islamogaming," *PC Magazine*, De-
                       cember 26, 2006.

Gary   "Life Is a Game," *Journal of Popular
Hoppenstand   Culture*, April 2006.

Reena Jana   "Enough with the Shoot-'em-Ups,"
                       Business Week, October 16, 2006.

Steven Levy   "Living a Virtual Life," *Newsweek*,
                       September 18, 2006.

William Lugo   "Violent Video Games Recruit
                       American Youth," *Reclaiming Children
                       & Youth*, Spring 2006.

Jessica Ramirez   "The New Ad Game," *Newsweek*, July
                       31, 2006.

James C. Rosser   "Nurse, Joystick!" *Atlantic Monthly*,
                       June 2007.

Marc Saltzman   "Video Games: A Force for Good?"
                       USA Today, August 15, 2006.

Seth Schiesel   "P.E. Classes Turn to Video Game
                       that Works Legs, Not Thumbs," *New
                       York Times*, April 30, 2007.

Mike Shields   "The Games Women Play," *Media
                       Week*, May 8, 2006.

Shawn Struck   "The Gaming Generation," *PC Maga-zine*, February 20, 2007.

Chris Suellentrop "Playing with Our Heads," *Wilson Quarterly*, Summer 2006.

Jeff Weinstock   "Too Late for the Revolution," *T.H.E. Journal*, April 2007.

Index